THE

SERPENT

&

THE

CROSS

Romel Duane Moore Sr.

Prayer Changes Things (PCT) Publishing
7551 Kingsport Road
Indianapolis, Indiana 46256

Scripture quotations are from the King James Version of the Bible, unless otherwise noted.

Cover design by Alexa Eliza.

For information contact:
Prayer Changes Things (PCT) Publishing
romel_moore@yahoo.com
(808) 371-0597

Printed in the United States of America.

Edited by Margaret Rose Mejia.

Hardcover ISBN: 979-8-9872375-2-6
Paperback ISBN: 979-8-9872375-3-3
Imprint: Independently Published

The name satan and the name baal are intentionally not capitalized.

C⊙NTENTS

DEDICATION

This book is dedicated to my cousin, Willie C. Pugh Jr.,
a.k.a. Thornton. When he left this world, he took
a part of us with him. He was one of the funniest
and talented humans God created.

INTRODUCTION

The enemy's introduction into mankind was not as satan, the devil, or the dragon. Man's archenemy made his grand entrance into the affairs of man as the serpent. The Law of First Mention dictates that the meaning of a thing when it first appears or is first mentioned in Scripture, maintains its meaning with every future occurrence. The devil is called "the serpent" in the Garden of Eden, not because he was transformed into a serpent in order to tempt Eve, and not because it is some fictional allegory to mystify what happened in the beginning with man. But satan was originally named the serpent when he first appeared because that is who and what God created him to be: the serpent. *The Serpent and The Cross* will re-present man's greatest nemesis in the light of Scripture. We will reexamine the biblical text and witness God's Spirit breathe afresh concerning the true identity of satan and unfold mysteries pertaining to the serpent and the journey of man from the Fall in the Garden of Eden to man's redemption at the Cross of Calvary. God's hidden wisdom was revealed and displayed when Jesus became sin, in order to destroy the power of sin.

I

THAT OLD SERPENT

Now the serpent was more subtil than any beast of the field which the LORD God had made...
Genesis 3:1

In the beginning, God originally created man in His image and after His likeness and gave man dominion over the Earth. God instructed Adam to be fruitful, multiply, replenish, subdue, and have dominion. God planted a garden eastward in Eden and instructed the first couple on Earth that they could eat of all the trees of the Garden of Eden. However, one of the two trees that was in the midst of the garden, the Tree of the Knowledge of Good and Evil, God strictly commanded that man could not eat of it, lest the day they ate, they would surely die. God intentionally withheld the knowledge of good and evil from Adam and Eve. This means that

6

unlike you and I and every human born into this world after the fall of man, God's first man and woman did not have an awareness of sin or a sin consciousness. Adam and Eve were not created perfectly. However, they were perfectly innocent. In order for man to face temptation absolutely unincumbered from any mitigating disadvantages, God created them without possessing a knowledge of good and evil. This presumption was that all they had to do was simply obey the one thing God instructed them not to do.

BLOODLINE

No one else but Adam could be responsible for this task of being obedient, not even Eve. God fully expected Eve to obey His Word as well, but the consequences of disobedience on all mankind fully rested upon Adam. In other words, if Eve had disobeyed God alone, but Adam had not, mankind would not have fallen and would still be in the Garden of Eden enjoying Paradise and life eternal. How so? First of all, Eve was not the head, Adam was. Second, Eve does not possess seed, only males have seed. Seed determines the bloodline, name, and identity of the family. God did not give woman the seed. He gave her a womb. This is why she is called woman, the combination of two words: womb, and man. She is the womb-man or woman. She is female, the combination of two words: fetus, and male. She is a fetus-male or female. Eve was an awesome creation to behold in her own right, but God never intended her to continue the name and bloodline of the human race. That responsibility fell on the shoulders of the man, Adam, alone.

God's purpose was for man to continue to duplicate His image and likeness in the Earth. If Eve, alone, had eaten from the forbidden tree and even fallen as a result, the future seed of man would not have fallen with her, and her fallen species would still be able to reproduce sinless, untainted sons and daughters of God, who would bear God's image and likeness in the Earth. How so? God did it with the virgin Mary. Mary was sinful, fallen, and in need of redemption.[1] But Jesus came from Heaven. He came from the Perfect Seed of God and although Mary was fallen, it was imperative that her womb was not tainted by fallen man and as a virgin she could receive Holy Seed, incubate it, and give birth to that which is holy, even though she was scarred by sin. God designed the reproductive organs of woman in such a way that the child she carries is a part of her and nourished by her, but completely separate from her, because the bloodline comes from the male. This is how God's image could have continued to be reproduced through Eve in a fallen state because it happened with Jesus' mother, Mary. The only one who determined whether mankind fell was Adam, because as the head, he possessed the seed and carried the bloodline.

THE HISSING ⊕NE

It was now test time for God's first man and woman. As a footnote, woman was not given the name Eve until after the Fall.[2] Before the Fall, the man's name was Adam and the woman's name was also Adam. Genesis 5:2 states, "...and (He) called their name Adam." For more about this, I refer you to my book, A Revelation of Eve. God did not bless man with Paradise and eternal life without being tested. Everything must be tested. If Adam passed the test, all of mankind would have been secure. If Adam failed the test, all of mankind would fall into sin. The enemy of man made his grand entrance into the life of man and chose to engage the woman, exclusively. This was very cunning and strategic, but before we delve into that, let's examine the serpent. First, we need to prove that satan is a serpent, and didn't just use the form of one to gain entrance, in order to communicate with Eve. As I meditated on this passage, something jumped out at me. One of the tasks of Adam was to name all of the animals. Since God gave Adam dominion over the Earth, it was logical that God would grant him the power to name the living creatures he had stewardship over. Naming the animals revealed that Adam possessed dominion over them. Whatever we name, we have power over. This is a universal principle. It was Adam who named all the fowl of the air, beasts of the field, and all that creeped upon the Earth. In other words, it was Adam who named the very one who was created as man's adversary. How do I know the Lord created the devil? Genesis 3:1a states, *"Now the serpent was more subtil than any beast of the field WHICH THE LORD GOD HAD MADE."* There you go: signed, sealed, and delivered.

Is the devil a serpent? Well Jesus informed us in Luke 10:19 that we would tread on serpents and scorpions, and over all the power of the enemy. Why is the Lord referring to the enemy as a "serpent" four thousand years after the enemy's appearance in the Garden of Eden? Maybe because that is who and what the devil is: a serpent. Greater understanding of this is revealed in Revelation 12:9:

And the great dragon was cast out, that old serpent, called the devil, and satan, which deceiveth the whole world . . .

The writer of Revelation refers to satan as *"that old serpent."* *Old* is the Greek word *archaios* meaning *original.*[3] It comes from the Greek root word *arche* meaning *a commencement, or (concretely) chief (of order, time, place, or rank): - beginning, first,* and *principality.*[4] It comes from another Greek root word *archomai* meaning, *precedence, to commence (in order of time): -* and *(rehearse from the) beginning.*[5] Scripture shows that he is a serpent, and he is called "the devil" and "satan." Therefore, "satan" and "the devil" is his name, but a serpent is what he is. Revelation 12:9 informs us how satan did not choose the body of a serpent just to gain access to man in the garden, but he was and is actually a serpent, and more importantly, he is *"the serpent."* He is called *"the old serpent"* because this word *old* literally means *original, beginning,* and *first and chief in order, time, place, and rank.* We now understand that satan is a literal serpent, and is the original serpent, the first serpent, the beginning serpent, the chief serpent, and commenced all other serpents and ranks as all serpents' principality. This changes the game! This is why we need to know our enemy. He desires to deceive us into believing he was once something holy, honorable, admired, powerful, and anointed. In addition, satan wants us to believe he was someone who once was beautiful and dwelt in the Presence of Almighty God. This is his greatest lie, and the Church fell for it hook, line, and sinker. He has always been and forever will be *"the serpent,"* not God's most beautiful angel, or an anointed cherub, or Heaven's worship leader, or Lucifer. The devil is the original serpent, and he did not fall into this state. He was created in this state. How do we know this to be true? John 8:44 says:

Ye are of your father the devil, and the lusts of your father ye will do. He was a murderer from the beginning, and abode not in the truth, because there is no truth in him. When he speaketh a lie, he speaketh of his own: for he is a liar, and the father of it.

1 John 3:8 states:

He that committed sin is of the devil; for the devil sinneth from the beginning . . .

Jesus is Creator. He made everything. So, He is the Authority on who was created, when something was created and what was created. The Creator said that satan was a *murderer* and *sinner* from the beginning. *Murderer* literally means *manslayer.*[6] This informs us that satan was not around eons and eons before the creation of man. satan was created specifically for man, so there would be no need for his existence before the existence of mankind. Jesus said that he was a murderer from the beginning. What beginning? His beginning as *"that old serpent,"* which means *beginning, original, first,* and *commencement.* The devil only had one beginning and it wasn't as Lucifer or some powerful, holy angel at God's Throne. His beginning was as the first serpent. Jesus said that the devil did not abide in the truth because there is no truth in him. Well, if the devil used to be the most beautiful angel in Heaven, he would have had some truth in him. If he were originally created as a holy cherub covering the very Throne of God, he would have had some truth in him. The Church has the devil's identity completely wrong. satan did not abide in the truth and he never worshipped at God's Throne. He was never holy, beautiful, and admired. He is the original serpent and was created infamously to do the very work he does at this moment and has always done from his beginning.

No Legs

After the fall of man, God showed up and began to hand out curses and consequences to everyone involved. Look at what God spoke to the serpent in Genesis 3:14:

And the LORD God said unto the serpent, Because thou hast done this, thou art cursed above all cattle, and above every beast of the field, upon thy belly shalt thou go, and dust shalt thou eat all the days of thy life.

There were repercussions for satan since he caused man to disobey God and these repercussions are very prophetic. The first thing God reiterates is that the serpent is a beast of the field. Let that sink in for a moment. The devil is a beast of the field. God told the serpent that upon his belly he would go.

This means serpents had legs and feet in the beginning. The punishment for his involvement in man's fall was the loss of his legs. What I want you to see here is that *"the old serpent,"* the first, original, and beginning serpent wasn't the only one cursed in this transaction, but all serpents were. Why were all serpents cursed? To this day, all serpents crawl upon their bellies and lick the dust of the earth. It is the same reason all humans born after Adam are born in sin and shapen in iniquity. It is because of the Fall and consequences of the first one. The devil is the first and original serpent, and God cursed the entire species because of the actions of the original serpent. Let that sink in.

The loss of legs signifies a fall. This means man was not the only one who fell in the Garden of Eden. God took the legs from the serpent because the serpent fell, also. This is very deep because the church teaches how satan fell from Heaven, assuming falling from Heaven dictates that satan fell from a holy realm. Heaven has many levels to it. We have the physical heavens where the sun, moon, and stars exist. The devil's position as the god of this world is a heavenly place where he is the prince of the power of the air.

Most times when we read the word *heaven* in Scripture it should be *heavens* (plural).[7] Genesis 1:1 says, *"In the beginning, God created the heaven (plural) and the earth."* Jesus came preaching, *"Repent: for the kingdom of heaven (plural) is at hand."* Jesus said that he beheld satan as lightning fall from heaven. When was this? It was in the garden when satan beguiled Eve into eating from the forbidden tree and she gave it to Adam to partake.

Broken Legs

Jesus was crucified between two thieves on Mount Calvary. These two men represent Adam and satan. Everything in Scripture means something. The left and right sides have meaning. The left side signifies the curse or what God has rejected, and the right side signifies the blessing or what (or who) God has accepted. In Jesus' *Parable of Wheat and Tares*, He said that the angels would separate the sheep nations on God's right side and the goat nations on God's left side. The thief on Jesus' left side represents the serpent and the thief on Jesus' right side represents Adam. During crucifixions, it took hours before the victims expired, and sometimes days. Since the Lord was crucified on a high holiday, the Roman soldiers had to expedite their deaths. Their bodies had to be dead and off the crosses by 3:00 p.m. In order to gasp for air during a crucifixion, one had to push up from his/her feet that were nailed to the cross in order to attempt to breathe properly. This of course, was excruciatingly painful. Because this was the only way for a person to continue breathing in order to stay alive, the soldiers would come and break the individuals' legs. This hindered the person from gasping for air.

The Roman soldiers came and broke the two thieves' legs. As aforementioned, the serpent lost his legs in the Garden of Eden representing his fall. This is reiterated at the crucifixion of Christ as the two thieves' legs were broken. Jesus was not a thief. He is the Giver of eternal life. The thief on the left represented satan of whom Jesus said, *"The thief cometh not, but for to steal, and to kill, and to destroy..."* The thief on Jesus' right side represented Adam, who stole fruit from the forbidden tree. When the Roman soldiers came to Jesus to break His legs, it was not necessary because the Lord had already died. They could not kill the Lord. Jesus said, *"No man taketh it (My Life) from me, but I lay it down of myself."* Jesus is Life. One cannot take His Life; He must give it willfully. The broken legs of the two thieves signified the Fall of both satan and Adam. The thief on the left is a picture of satan because that thief was impenitent, and he ridiculed the Lord during the crucifixion. The thief on the left, the cursed side, had his legs broken, lost his legs, and experienced his fall in the Garden of Eden when he got man to disobey God and eat from the forbidden tree. The thief on the right, the side of blessing, is a picture of Adam as he repented and recognized the Lord as the sinless One from Heaven. Concerning the thief on the left, his fall is eternal. Regarding the thief on the right, his fall was not eternal because Jesus died for man's sins and when we repent and acknowledge the sacrifice of Jesus for our sins, we are forgiven and receive access to eternal life.

BACK TO PARADISE

After the thief on the right repented to the Lord Jesus said something very prophetic to him. Luke 23:43 says:

And Jesus said unto him, Verily I say unto thee, Today shalt thou be with me in paradise.

Jesus did not just extend forgiveness to the penitent malefactor on His right side, but the Lord also added how that very day (upon his death) he would be with Christ in Paradise. What is Paradise? Paradise is the Garden of Eden. The same garden where the first Adam sinned and fell, the second Adam came, paid the price for our sins, and redeemed and restored us back to it. The garden was planted eastward in Eden and Eden is Heaven. Jesus literally redeemed us back to where we were before the Fall. This means that we fell from Heaven (Heavenly places) because the garden was in Eden. This also means when the serpent fell and lost his legs, he fell from Heaven, also. Therefore, when Jesus states, "I beheld satan, as lightning fall from Heaven." He was speaking concerning the

19

serpent's fall in the Garden of Eden, when he lost his legs, which signifies a fall.

Sonic Hedgehog Gene

Snakes originally had complete forelimbs and hindlimbs. If you look carefully at the tail end of most serpents, you will see the rudiments of its legs. There is a tiny spur protruding that looks like a dark brown spot.[8] To discover why snakes no longer develop limbs, scientists researched the genetic circuit that controls limb development. They compared the genetic circuits of a lizard that develops limbs and a python that does not develop limbs. The scientists identified a break in the circuit in which an important gene called the "Sonic Hedgehog" (that is required for limb development), only flickers on and then goes off in the python. Whereas in any other creature, the Sonic Hedgehog (SHH) gene stays on and acts as the motor that drives limb development all the way down to the fingers and the toes. They found there are three mutations that occur, not in the SHH gene itself, but in an enhancer, a switch that controls when the SHH gene turns on and switches off.

These mutations are responsible for the very weak activity of the gene.

The enhancer switch flickers on and off because the activators of that gene are not able to bind and switch on transcription. In serpents, the SHH gene flickers on and within twenty-four hours it turns off. This has boggled the minds of scientists and they mark it up as a strange evolution in snakes.[9] However, God's Word is Truth, and it reveals the "when" and "why" of this mystery in snakes. It happened in the Garden of Eden when the original serpent beguiled Eve to eat from the forbidden tree. Part of the Divine judgement for satan's involvement in the fall of man, was the loss of his limbs and this judgement was also for all future serpents. In other words, when the Creator spoke the words, *"upon thy belly shalt thou go"* there was a mutation in the enhancer of the Sonic Hedgehog gene which made it work only long enough (twenty-four hours), leaving just enough evidence (a tiny claw) for us to realize that limbs use to grow here but somehow stopped. This is why we should never look for God in science but look to the God of science. It may take science thousands of years to uncover what God said was true in Scripture.

LICK THE DUST

The second part of the serpent's Divine judgement was being cursed to lick the dust of the earth. This is even more impressive than the permanent malfunction of the Sonic Hedgehog gene in snakes. If God cursed the serpent to begin to lick the dust of the earth, that means serpents did not do this before. It was at this moment when serpents' tongues were split and became forked. At the same time, within the roof of their mouths something called "the Jacobson's organ" was developed. The Jacobson's organ is shaped identically to the forked tongue and each time the forked tongue re-enters the mouth, it slides into the perfectly fitted Jacobson's organ where information is retrieved and analyzed.[10]

The way that humans smell is by sniffing scent particles from the air and discerning them. Snakes do this very differently. They stick their moist forked tongue out to gather scent particles. In other words, their tongues literally lick the dust of the earth. When their forked tongue is brought in, it connects with their Jacobson's organ and retrieves the scent particles. Then, the forked tongue puts the scent particles in direct contact with their sensory organs. This makes their sense of smell hundreds of times more sensitive than ours. So, each time a snake's tongue flickers, it is licking the dust of the earth and gathering information about its environment so that it can decide what it needs to do next.

JACOBSON'S ⊕RGAN

It is not a coincidence that the organ the serpent's forked tongue returns to, in order to interpret the dust particles, is called "Jacobson's organ." The name *Jacob* means *supplanter, heel catcher, liar in wait,* and *layer of snares,* and it comes from a Hebrew root word meaning *circumvent, follow at the heel, assail insidiously, overreach, to come from behind, to defraud,* and *to hold back.*[11] Jacob in Scripture came out his mother's womb holding the heel of his elder twin brother, Esau, and later on would cheat and steal his brother's firstborn blessing. Jacob lied in wait, supplanted, circumvented, assailed insidiously, overreached, came from behind, and defrauded his brother. Likewise, this is the nature of the serpent in relation to mankind. He is our "heel catcher" and daily lays snares for us. One of the ways he accomplishes his evil agenda is through his forked tongue. However, his forked tongue cannot function properly without Jacobson's organ.

I want you to notice that the serpent was cursed to lick the dust of the earth and man's flesh was made from the dust of the earth. Therefore, the serpent's diet is our flesh. The serpent and the flesh (the carnal mind and carnal lusts) are connected. The serpent has instant access to every part of our life that is carnal, earthly, and sinful. Now we understand the Apostle Paul's reasoning when he admonishes us not to "fulfil the lust of the flesh," but to "Walk in the Spirit" (Galatians 5:16). Ephesians 4:27 instructs us not to give place to the devil. One of the greatest ways we "give place to the devil" is by walking in the flesh and doing the things that are dirty, carnal, and lack true spiritual integrity. The serpent's diet is the dust of the earth and that is the flesh.

THE SERPENT & THE CROSS

Antaeus & Hercules

In Greek mythology there was a person named Antaeus who would challenge all passer-by to wrestling matches. He was undefeated as long as he remained touching the earth for his power came from the earth, his mother. He successfully pinned his opponents to the ground and killed them. As Hercules was on his way to the Garden of Hesperides as his eleventh labor, he encountered Antaeus and they fought. Hercules could not defeat Antaeus by wrestling and pinning him so, he lifted Antaeus from the earth in a bear hug and crushed him to death.

This mythological story gives us glimpses of prophetic truth. Antaeus is a type of the serpent because its strength is its ability to lick the dust of the earth and man's flesh is made (birthed) from the earth. Antaeus strength was the earth and the serpent's power comes from being connected to the earthly man of our flesh and everything that is earthly, worldly, sinful and carnal. Hercules is a type of Christ because Hercules father was Zeus so he was half god and half human. Jesus, the Only Begotten Son, came from the Father and is one hundred percent God and one hundred percent man. Hercules was on his way to the Garden of Hesperides for his eleventh labor and Jesus came to earth on His Journey to the Garden of Eden (Abraham's bosom – Hades) to deliver all the souls who remained there in wait for their salvation by Christ the Messiah. This was Christ's labor, to die for the sins of the whole world. This is why its called the "work of Calvary." It was Christ who gave the serpent its power therefore He knew exactly how to defeat him. On the Cross, Jesus was crucified being lifted up and suspended between Heaven and Earth. When He became sin for man and was elevated from the earth, as Hercules defeated Antaeus by lifting him from the earth in a bear hug, crushing him; Jesus crushed the serpents head when he was lifted up on the Cross as the Sacrifice for our sins thereby crushing the power of sin and defeating satan at the same time, once and for all.

II

THE SERPENT'S TONGUE

erpent is the Hebrew word *nakas* meaning *a snake (from its hiss):-serpent.*[1] It comes from the root word *nachash* meaning *to hiss, whisper (a magic spell): to prognosticate; enchanter,* and *to practice divination.*[2] This is a very important insight if we are going to understand the power of the enemy. His most effective ability is as the serpent, the one who hisses, and whispers a magic spell. He knows the power of words and uses them deceptively and with evil intent. His words are like divination to the hearers. *Prognosticate* means *to foretell or prophesy (an event in the future).* It means *foretell from signs or symptoms, predict,* and *to give an indication of in advance.*[3] This is what the serpent was doing to Eve: hissing and whispering his lies that were like magic and spells. The serpent was enchanting her and attempting to foretell and prophesy her future. *"Now the serpent was more subtil than any beast of the field..."* Subtil is the Hebrew word *arum* meaning *cunning, crafty,* and *prudent.*[4] It comes from the root word *aram* meaning *to make bare (through the idea, perhaps of smoothness)* and *to be cunning.*[5] The whole purpose of the serpent was to communicate with Eve and to practice divination on her through his words. The serpent's words would cause her to disobey God and that would result in her being made bare. This is exactly what transpired as she gave attention to the slickster's words. She ate the fruit and gave it to Adam to partake of it, also. Their eyes were opened, and they knew they were naked. Ashamed, they ran to make aprons of fig leaves.

MIXING GOOD & EVIL

As we examine the forked tongue of the serpent, it speaks directly to the power and way satan uses words. Serpents have one tongue with two endings. This is prophetic of how his tongue speaks. He mixes good and evil, light and darkness, truth and lies, and right and wrong. The serpent's power is his ability to mix God's truth with lies. This is how he casts a magic spell on the masses. Synonyms of the word *mix* are *fuse, combine, mingle, blend, incorporate,* and *merge.*[6] The serpent's forked tongue mixes, fuses, combines, mingles, blends, incorporates, and merges a little bit of the truth with absolute lies and he is able to beguile and seduce most of humanity. The only tree Adam and Eve were forbidden to eat from in the Garden of Eden was called the Tree of the Knowledge of Good and Evil. This tree is symbolic of the serpent's tongue. It is one tree with two knowledges: good and evil, (one tongue with two endings). This tree possesses good, and this is how so many people get entangled in its web. Most of humanity will not blindly follow pure evil and the serpent understands this. Therefore, his strength is in his ability to mix some good with what is evil, and that will still result in death.

The Catholic Church does not openly advertise paganism, sodomy, and idol worship. However, what we initially see and hear about Catholicism is the good: hospitals, orphanages, and schools. There are a lot of good works performed by each archdiocese. However, at Catholicism's core is the forbidden abomination of praying to and for dead people, and a false priesthood with "priests" who have taken unrealistic vows of abstinence from sex because Catholic "priests" are also not allowed to marry. This opens demonic doors to pedophilia and homosexuality. Another sinful practice in the Catholic Church is confessing one's sins to men (who are not graced and ordained by God to be mediators for God) because there is only One Mediator between God and man, Yeshua our Lord (1 Timothy 2:5). The Catholic Church boasts a membership of about one billion followers, while many of their fundamental practices are clearly prohibited by the Bible they are supposed to obey.

Another great example of the power of the serpent's tongue (that mixes good and evil) is the celebration of Christmas and Easter. Anyone can Google the history of these two major holidays, and the internet will educate a person concerning the pagan origins of Christmas and Easter. It will explain how the Catholic Church mixed known pagan practices with sacred biblical ones and how these holidays became known as Christmas and Easter. These holidays are an abomination of the true worship of the Most High God. Yahweh gave His people seven major holidays to celebrate in Scripture.[7] However, somehow the serpent was successful in getting the Church to totally neglect these biblical "holy-days" and fully celebrate two pagan days that have nothing to do with the Bible. If you attempt to enlighten so-called "Christians" about the truth behind Christmas and Easter, you will get a crash course in the serpent's forked tongue that can cast a magic spell. People will tell you "straight up" how they will never give up celebrating Christmas. The serpent was cunning enough to put children at the heart of this pagan worship with gifts and stockings for the children at Christmas, Easter eggs and baskets for the children at Easter, and trick-or-treat candy and children's costumes for Halloween. The serpent mixed, fused, mingled, blended, and incorporated some good with his evil, a little truth with his big lies, a portion of light with his darkness, some Bible with a lot of paganism, and even the Church of the Lord fell for it, "hook, line and sinker." This is what happened at the Tree of the Knowledge of Good and Evil. The serpent strategized his battle at this tree because it signified his very nature. In Genesis 3:4-5, the serpent mixed a little bit of the truth with the lie:

And the serpent said unto the woman, Ye shall not surely die:

For God doth know that in the day ye eat thereof, then your eyes shall be opened, and ye shall be as gods, knowing good and evil.

The serpent lied about how man would not surely die, but he told the truth of how man would be as gods as their eyes would be opened to know good and evil. The enemy has no new tricks up his sleeve. He simply regurgitates the same ole playbook he has used from the beginning because that is the only power he possesses – the forked tongue.

God Hates a Mixture

God's Law gives specific instructions concerning mixtures. The purpose of these instructions is to signify the unlawfulness of mixing natures or spirits. Deuteronomy 22:9-11 says:

Thou shalt not sow thy vineyard with divers seeds: lest the fruit of thy seed which thou hast sown, and the fruit of thy vineyard, be defiled.

Thou shalt not plow with an ox and an ass together.

Thou shalt not wear a garment of divers sorts, as of woollen and linen together.

Two different kinds of seeds, an ox and ass, and two different garments, wool and linen are all prophetic of two types of natures. Planting two kinds of seeds in one field speaks concerning two types of natures in one person. An ox is a picture of the spirit of man because it is powerful and can carry great burdens. The ass is prophetic of the flesh because it is rebellious and stiff-necked. These two beasts signify the two natures: spirit and flesh. They are opposite and oppose each other. This is the battleground of mankind. We are born fallen and possess the sinful nature of the ass. However, when we accept the sacrifice of Christ on Calvary's Cross, we are Born Again and receive the new nature, God's Divine Nature. This is the dichotomy of man. But the Scripture is clear: bitter and sweet water cannot come from the same fountain. Once we are Born Again, it is our responsibility to study, learn, and allow the Holy Spirit to guide us into understanding the new Divine Nature we inherited when we received salvation. Jesus said that people do not put new wine into old wineskins. Once we receive the new wineskin of the regenerated, Born Again spirit, God is able to pour the new wine of His Spirit into us. Every Believer who does not discover the awesomeness of walking in the Spirit and what it truly means (that the Kingdom of God is within us), will live a limited, defeated, and frustrated life, even though Jesus has given us everything pertaining to life and godliness. It is our daily assignment to mortify the deeds and nature of the carnal man and reveal and free the deeds and nature of our spirit man.

God forbade the mixing of seeds in a field, and the mixing of different fabrics in a garment because it pointed to mixing natures (spiritually): light and darkness, good and evil, and truth and lies. He knew this was the strategy of the serpent and its forked tongue. So, God revealed this truth in the beginning, prohibiting man to eat from a tree that possessed the knowledge of good and evil. This universal truth rings true every single day we eat from this tree of mixture, we surely die. This truth does not pertain to the mixing of races because all races are of the human race and does not constitute a different nature. But as it is clearly seen in Genesis chapter six, it is an abomination to mix angelic seed with human seed. This is why their offspring were unnatural and called "giants." As a result of their actions (mixing angelic and human DNA), they reaped the consequences, a worldwide flood and the destruction of these hybrid, evil creatures.

III

SPELLBOUND

During the temptation of Jesus, something interesting was stated by satan without any objection by the Lord. Luke 4:5-6 records:

And the devil, taking him up into an high mountain, shewed unto him all the kingdoms of the world in a moment of time.

And the devil said unto him, All this power will I give thee, and the glory of them: for that is delivered unto me; and to whomsoever I will I give it.

It is no coincidence the enemy's showdown with Jesus took place in the wilderness. I love this definition of wilderness: *A neglected or abandoned area of a garden or town.*[1] The first Adam failed during the serpent's temptation in the Garden of Eden. This temptation was in three areas: the lust of the eyes, the lust of the flesh, and the pride of life.

THE SERPENT & THE CROSS

Jesus came as the "Last Adam" and undoubtedly would be tempted in the same three areas. They are no longer in the Garden of Eden, but because of the Fall, the fallen world we were cast into was now *a neglected or abandoned area of a garden.* The world as we know it is a wilderness, and in the wilderness, serpents are much more plenteous. satan is the god of this world and 1 John 2:16 reminds us:

For all that is in the world, the lust of the flesh, and the lust of the eyes, and the pride of life, is not of the Father, but is of the world.

The question we must ask is, "How did satan become the god of this world?" The devil answered it in the day he tempted the Lord. He said ". . . *for that is delivered unto me . . .*" Delivered is the Greek word *peradidomi* meaning *to surrender,* for example: *yield up, entrust, transmit: - betray, bring forth, give over, and put in prison.*[2] It means *to give to the hands of another. To give over into one's power or use. To deliver to someone to keep, use, take care of,* and *manage.* The Church teaches that Adam forfeited the authority God gave him over the Earth, and by default handed it over to the serpent, the one who caused him to fall. However, when we read the biblical account, both man and the serpent fell at the same time. Man fell from his spiritual position of righteousness and authority in God and the serpent lost his legs. Adam's spiritual eyes were closed, and his carnal eyes were opened with the Fall. The serpent lost his legs, and was cursed to crawl upon his belly, and eat the dust of the earth. This signified a similar reality. What happened in the Garden of Eden was different from the rule in the movie *Chronicles of Riddick* where the necromancers lived by the rule, "You keep what you kill." The serpent did not keep what he killed or caused to fall because he could never have God's Spirit, bare God's image, and likeness, and receive God's righteousness. He could never be bone of God's Bone and flesh of His Flesh. He could never sit at the right hand of the Father. However, even though the serpent fell, he did receive management over what the Scripture describes as the cosmos. He is the god of this world. World does not mean Earth.

SPELLBOUND

The power of the *nâchash* as *the hissing one, who whispers, casts spells,* and *works divination through his words* is the opposite of God's nature and the power of His Words. Life and death are in the power of the tongue. God's Word gives life and satan uses words to produce death. Jesus is the Word of God, and all things were made by Him. If the Word of God made everything, this means the very core of all creation contains the mystery of the power of God's Word. All creation (spiritual and physical) exists by this phenomenon. The book of Hebrews informs us that the worlds were framed by the Word of God. Words are the essence of all things which means words inherently have the ability to initiate change at any given moment. Words spoken can encourage and uplift one's spirit or words spoken can tear down and break one's heart. The tongue possesses the power of life and death. A grade schoolteacher can publicly tell a child that he or she is stupid and "will never amount to anything in life" or the teacher can publicly celebrate the child and declare that he/she "can do anything they put their mind to."

The serpent goes about attempting to pervert everything God has created, especially God's highest creation of man. He does this by using the same process God used to create man; satan uses words. Unfortunately, the serpent understands the power, potential, and purpose of words better than God's Church. He is a master-manipulator of words, but Jesus is the Word of God. The serpent perverts words and turns them inside-out in order to manifest evil in the Earth. We see this in operation with Eve at the Tree of the Knowledge of Good and Evil. The serpent used his expertise to extrapolate God's Word to the woman and inserted enough doubt and misinformation to render the optimal outcome. When you read their conversation, you are hearing sorcery at its highest level. God's Word was delivered to man and the serpent used words to convince man that the words they heard meant something quite different. This was a master's class in divination and casting spells.

THE SERPENT & THE CROSS

SPELLING

I was having a conversation with my eldest son about this, and he spontaneously replied, "This is why it is called spelling." The very act of writing words is called "spelling." Words by nature cast a spell. *Spell* means to name or write the letters of in order.[3] Simply naming the letters for a word is called "spell." God designed words by nature to make us spellbound. The serpent taps into this power, perverts it, and uses it for evil rather than good. He uses it to destroy man and manifest the worst in humanity. Words are necessary to execute dominion and it was never intended to be used against man but for man to use to maintain dominion over Earth.

God gave dominion over the planet to man who has His Spirit and bears His image and likeness. In the beginning, Adam and Eve had God's Spirit and bore His image and likeness and everything functioned in perfect harmony as God intended. When man fell by eating from the forbidden tree, they lost God's Spirit and no longer bore His image and likeness. This means there was no one to manage the world and to this end, God allowed the serpent to take up management and he became the god of this world. But when man fell, it not only affected man, but all of creation fell with man. Paul explains this in Romans 8:19-22 NLT:

For all creation is waiting eagerly for that future day when God will reveal who his children really are.

Against its will, all creation was subjected to God's curse. But with eager hope,

the creation looks forward to the day when it will join God's children in glorious freedom from death and decay.

For we know that all creation has been groaning as in the pains of childbirth right up to the present time.

We do not know what man and creation actually looked like and how it functioned before the Fall. Everything was cursed and affected by the Fall. Man, no longer had the ability to govern the planet as God originally intended. God equipped Adam and Eve to govern and have dominion as they stood in His righteousness. However, when they fell, man lost his rightful position in God to rule. When this world was cursed and fell into a fallen, sinful, lower dimension of existence, the serpent became the god of that world. For this reason, I state that we did not give the devil our authority in the Fall, but in essence, we fell into his authority. When Adam and Eve's eyes were opened and they knew they were naked, it was their natural, physical, carnal eyes that were opened. Their eyes were opened to the fallen, sinful, cursed world where the serpent is the god. In the garden, the serpent had to submit to man's authority as the ruler over the planet. After the Fall, man had to submit to the authority of the serpent as the ruler because creation no longer existed from the same dimension.

In the beginning, when Adam was full of God's Spirit and had God's image and likeness, Adam exercised his dominion by the use of words. That is how God designed Adam. It was God's Word that brought the world into existence, and it would be words that governed God's world. This could only happen as man was filled with the Holy Ghost and had God's image. This means our ability to govern and walk in dominion is directly connected to being righteous (in right standing) with God and possessing His Spirit and image. In this condition, when Adam spoke, God spoke. All things were made by God's Word and naturally obeyed His Voice. The only way to possess God's Voice is to have His Word and His Spirit. Adam manifested his dominion over the earth through the vehicle of words. We call it communication, not from barking like dogs, purring like cats, or mooing like cows, but from the advanced art and ability to use words.

After man fell, Paul informs us how creation was made subject to vanity and decay because of the curse. Creation hates that it is now under the temporary management of the serpent. Creation was designed to respond to God's Voice and His Words. But in this fallen dispensation, creation is made subject to a destructive tyrant who only desires to kill, steal, and destroy. God did not intend creation to form tornadoes, thunderstorms, tsunamis, hurricanes, or destructive weather conditions. However, creation fell when man fell and is now made to be governed by the evil one. This is fascinating because Apostle Paul explains how creation actually groans waiting for the manifestation of the sons of God. In other words, creation desperately yearns to return to the management of man who bears God's image, has His Spirit, and speaks the very words of God because God's Word is truth, light, wholesome, righteous, and excellent.

WIND & WATER

An awesome example of this truth is seen in the story of Jesus walking on water in Matthew 14. Jesus sent the disciples before Him by boat to the other side of the sea. Jesus then came walking on the water and would have walked right past the boat with the disciples if they had not called out to Him. They were afraid because of the storm. What does a storm consist of? Storms consist of intense winds upon the water. The storm that the disciples were afraid of was actually creation celebrating the Presence of its Creator. The wind knew who Jesus was. The sea recognized the Lord and in exuberant celebration the wind and the sea began shouting for the Only Begotten Son of God and formed an aquatic conveyor belt for the Lord to personally escort him to the other side of the sea. Jesus literally walked from one great wave to another. Paul exclaimed that creation is groaning, waiting for the manifestation of the sons of God. Jesus said that the works He did, we would also do, because He was leaving to go to His Father. This is the awesome position and power the Lord redeemed and restored us back to through His death and resurrection.

Although satan is the god of this world, creation does not want to submit to him because he is a destroyer and does not use words from its original intended position and power. Although creation was naturally designed to respond to God's Word, for the last six thousand years, creation was made subject to vanity and decay. It is under a perpetual curse and under the management of he who perverts. Creation desires to respond to God's Voice, not the one who hisses, whispers witchcraft, and speaks divination. We are in this world but not of it. Our kingdom is higher, and our heavenly kingdom exists on a higher spiritual dimension. Everyone who repents and accepts Christ in their hearts has a regenerated spirit in God's image and likeness and God positions them back in His righteousness (right standing with God). At this point, they are operating from the position and authority that the first Adam possessed. The second Adam came to seek and save that which was lost. Once we are Born Again, we have God's Spirit and bear His image and likeness. He has given us His

Word. Why do we need His Word? Because the worlds were framed by the Word of God and as we mature in the things of God, He begins to trust us with walking in this awesome authority. As we speak God's Word, creation will happily obey because it is groaning, waiting for us to come into full maturity as sons of God, not babes in Christ, but mature sons of God who understand who they are in Christ and how God originally designed this to work. Sons of God can be trusted with the responsibility of being led by the Spirit of God and speaking His Word to destroy the works of the devil and establish and advance the Kingdom of God. Sons of God sit at the feet of Jesus and learn the keys of the kingdom, and how to lock, unlock, bind, and loose. Sons of God are those who desire the mysteries of the kingdom concerning the power of God's Word and begin to change and take authority over the things the serpent's tongue has hissed, whispered, and cast an evil, demonic spell over in creation. Sons of God correct blind eyes, crippled bodies, mentally ill minds, and demon possessed and oppressed humans. And sons of God are regulated by the power of God's spoken Word.

GOD'S SPELL

After Christ died on the Cross for the sins of the world and was resurrected for our justification, He ascended to Heaven and sent His Spirit to live within every Believer. In this new, recreated position and power, there was a paradigm shift in the Earth. Therefore, Jesus commanded his followers, now called "His Body" and "The Church," to preach this unique message of the Kingdom of Heaven and He called it "The Gospel." *Gospel* literally means *God's spell*. The word *gospel* is derived from the Anglo-Saxon term *god-spell*, meaning, *good story*, a rendering of the Latin *evangelium* and the Greek *evangelion*, meaning *good news or good telling*.[4] God designed it that when His Born-Again creation uses His gift of speech through words to communicate the message of the Word of God (Who came and died for our sins), His Spirit would cause a Divine "God-spell" upon the hearers. This "God-spell" is necessary because those who hear the gospel are spiritually dead and incapable of understanding the message because it is spiritual in nature, and the natural man cannot receive the things of God, neither can he know them because they are spiritually discerned. So, God's Spirit supernaturally causes a "God-spell" upon the hearers of the message of the Kingdom and their eyes, ears, and hearts are opened to fully understand God's boundless love in the sacrifice of Christ for our sins. This is the miracle of salvation, and it was designed this way from the beginning. The serpent has power, but God is all powerful. The serpent's forked tongue is formidable, but Jesus is the Word of God and God has magnified His Word above His Name!

Isn't it interesting how many of the infamous personalities who originated evil theories and practices denounced the very evil they created before their deaths? Darwin denounced the theory of evolution before he died.[5] The infamous "Roe" (Norma McCorvey) in Roe v. Wade denounced the murder of innocent life in the womb before she died.[6] Al Gore learned about "global warming" as a theory in college from Professor Roger Revelle, who was the professor who started measuring CO_2 in the atmosphere. When Revelle was a visiting professor at Harvard University, he taught a course on "greenhouse warming." Al Gore took the course as a freshman and received a "D." Despite Gore's grade and lack of knowledge on the subject, somehow Gore became the foremost authority on the subject of "global warming" shortly thereafter. His professor denounced "global warming" as any authentic foundation of real scientific knowledge.[7] However, the traffickers, charlatans, and opportunists denounced Professor Revelle and proceeded to spread their lies and disinformation because it became a religion for them, and after "global warming" was debunked, they are presently deceiving the world under a new term "climate change" as if climates aren't supposed to change.

IV

BLACK MAMBA BABEL

Shortly after the destruction of the known world by God's Divine judgment (by the Flood in Noah's day), the serpent was back at work. God sent a worldwide flood and swept away all the serpent's wickedness that he had planted in the Earth. The serpent could not wait to implement another diabolical scheme to pay God back for extinguishing his demonic hybrid of giants that came from the ungodly union and crossbreeding of angels and humans recorded in Genesis chapter six. This plot came to a head in the building of the city and Tower of Babel. Genesis 11:1-4 records:

And the whole earth was of one language, and of one speech.

And it came to pass, as they journeyed from the east, that they found a plain in the land of Shinar; and they dwelt there.

And they said one to another, Go to, let us make brick, and burn them thoroughly. And they had brick for stone, and slime had they for morter.

And they said, Go to, let us build us a city and a tower, whose top may reach unto heaven; and let us make us a name, lest we be scattered abroad upon the face of the whole earth.

Before God confounded the languages, the earth was of one language, and one speech. Language is the Hebrew word *sapa* and it is literally translated *lip* in 112 other places in Scripture.[1] It is only used for the word *language* seven times. It is defined as, *the lip (as a natural boundary), a margin (of a vessel, water, or cloth) – bank, brink, border, brim, edge, shore, speech,* and *talk.* Speech is the Hebrew word *dabar* meaning *a word, a matter (as spoken of) or thing, an act, advice, affair,* and *answer.*[2] The same Hebrew word is translated *word* 807 times. The Earth was of one lip and one word. This is an enormously powerful reality. It is one thing for everyone to speak the same language. However, for everyone to say the same thing, it shows us that the serpent was able to convince Nimrod, and the entire population to turn against God for destroying their forefathers. The enemy used Nimrod, the first world leader after the flood, to preach this message of rebellion. The serpent's forked tongue was so effective that they galvanized behind this in one word: rebel. They were of "one lip." The shore is "the lip" for the incoming tide of the ocean. It serves as the boundary, brink, brim, and edge. On the mouth, the lip serves as the boundary for the tongue and for our speech. In other words, words must cross the natural boundary of the lips on the mouth before speech is released and heard. The Earth had "one lip." They were not of differing opinions and messages. They believed and said the same thing without the difficulty of having to communicate with people of many different languages.

This is what the serpent is attempting to do in this "plan-demic" season through the use of censorship, intimidation, and the "cancel culture." They want to shame you into complying, and obeying their demonic, perverse ideology. The "Big Tech" Companies and mainstream media is an extension of the serpent's forked tongue. His false prophets of baal arrogantly sit in their seats of disinformation and put fear and lies on the air, daily, brainwashing the sheepish nature of the world. The serpent doesn't care if its socialism or communism, as long as it is not freedom. Free people cannot be controlled, and the serpent's ultimate goal is obedience. Freedom is one of the most powerful forces on earth. We are free to eat what we want, say what we want, vote how we want, and more importantly, think how we want. Daily, we are witnessing the decay of freedom in America. The devil isn't hiding anymore, and the masses still do not see him. The serpent is openly using strongarm tactics on anyone who has the courage to speak against his "plan-demic," and it is amazing how silent millions of Americans have become.

There is an old saying, *"History repeats itself because we were not paying attention the first time."* We are witnessing the re-introduction of the serpent's rebellion against God in the rebuilding of his Tower of Babel. What is very scary about the first building of the Tower of Babel is what God said concerning the people:

And the LORD said, Behold, the people is one, and they have all one language; and this they begin to do: and now nothing will be restrained from them, which they have imagined to do.

Go to, let us go down, and there confound their language, that they may not understand one another's speech.
Genesis 11:6-7

God Himself declared that as long as the people had one language and were one, nothing would be restrained from them which they imagined doing. One of their purposes was to make a name for themselves. *Name* is the Hebrew word *sem* meaning, *definite and conspicuous position as a mark or memorial of individuality – reputation, glory, by implication – honor, authority, character, fame, monument, renown, and report.*[3] The serpent had convinced the people to desire to make a name, position as a mark, or memorial for themselves as they rebelled against God. They desired to be infamous throughout history, and to gain glory, honor, and a reputation concerning the report of how they unified to say and do as one people. God said, "...*nothing would be restrained from them.*" *Restrained* is the Hebrew word *basar* meaning *to clip off, to gather grapes, to be isolated (inaccessible by height or fortification); cut off, and (de) fenced.*[4] In essence, God admitted that nothing would be inaccessible, fortified, or defensed from them. What a statement. God's intent when He created man was for us to live without limitation in the faith realm where all things are possible. Pentecost is the positive parallel to the Tower of Babel. However, the serpent was able to get man to accomplish this great feat through the perversion of what God originally purposed. Notice, it all began with language and the power of words.

BABYLON

Babylon comes from the name *Babel* and *Babel* means *gate of baal, confusion, chaos, nothingness,* and *vanity*.[5] The beginning of home computers was led by two great names: Bill Gates of *Microsoft* and *Gateway* Computers. Is this a coincidence? Never. The serpent was ready to repeat his rebellion of the building of the Tower of Babel and it would begin at the "gate of baal." Bill Gates not only led the way in computer technology but presently is in the forefront of the "global reset," which this "plan-demic" is all about. The computer case that holds many components of a personal or office desktop is called a "tower." Computer technology has become the new gate into man's ears, eyes, and mind. As we enjoy the entertainment and comfort of computers and technology, there is a sinister agenda at the heart of this technology. The serpent desires to bring the world back to one language and speech, and it is being accomplished through computer science and the internet, also known as the information highway, worldwide web, the net, and cyberspace. Cabal is the one language, and one speech the serpent's forked tongue will use to build his new rebellious Tower of Babel in order to usher in mass destruction and chaos.

The purpose of the Tower of Babel was to reach the heavens. They desired to reach Heaven because Divine judgment that destroyed their forefathers came from Heaven. Under Nimrod, they had one mind to physically attack God in Heaven. Through the technology of today, the serpent uses the airwaves of "heaven" to communicate and transmit information via our smart phones and the internet. Ultimately, in the end, the enemy will attempt to do the same thing they wanted to do in Genesis eleven: bombard Heaven to overthrow it. Through artificial intelligence and the advanced technology of today, the Book of Revelation has already foretold that satan will finally have his day when he will invade Heaven. Revelation 12:7-9 records:

And there was war in heaven: Michael and his angels fought against the dragon; and the dragon fought and his angels,

And prevailed not; neither was their place found any more in heaven.

And the great dragon was cast out, that old serpent, called the devil, and satan, which deceiveth the whole world: he was cast out into the earth, and his angels were cast out with him.

What Nimrod and the people of earth attempted to do in Genesis chapter eleven will be accomplished. However, they will fail horribly again. It will occur very soon with the anti-Christ when the events of Revelation chapter twelve transpire.

THE TOWER

The rebellious renegade who craved revenge for the deaths of their lineage during the flood built a tower. We've discussed how our computers have towers but if we dig a little deeper, we will discover a more diabolical revelation. Tower comes from a Hebrew root word *gaw-dal* meaning *to be (or make) large, (as in body, mind, state, honor, or pride); advance, boast, bring up, exceed, make (wax) great, increase, lift up, magnify,* and *tower.*[6] The word *tower* literally describes the mentally deranged personality of the one who will attempt such an insane feat of actually storming the abode of Almighty God. The serpent who will possess the body of the anti-Christ will reach a point in his own mind that he will lift himself up, boast, and magnify himself. Daniel 11:36 describes him:

And the king shall do according to his will; and he shall exalt himself, and magnify himself above every god, and shall speak marvellous things against the God of gods, and shall prosper till the indignation be accomplished: for that that is determined shall be done.

The tower that is built to reach into Heaven is the tower of pride, and arrogance in our own minds.

This is the same tower the forked-tongued serpent used to beguile Eve. The serpent stated to her in Genesis 3:4-5:

And the serpent said unto the woman, Ye shall not surely die:

For God doth know that in the day ye eat thereof, then your eyes shall be opened, and ye shall be as gods, knowing good and evil.

This tower of pomposity is vividly at work today in those who call themselves "the elite." Their ideology is called "Wokeism." They live in a bubble of egotistical stupidity where they pass laws and create rules, wherein, they never obey these laws and rules, themselves. They publicly demand everyone to wear masks when they themselves never intend to wear them. They pass legislation demanding your children to stay home from school, and do remote learning that does not work, while their children attend private schools. They are serpents, hypocrites, and the worst of humanity. They believe they are gods and rules do not apply to them. They also believe that they should be the ones in power to make the rules for everyone else who exists beneath them. However, pride goes before destruction and a haughty look before a fall. This evil mindset comes from their father, the devil, and he will be the one who finally takes the step of faith in the insanity of believing he can overthrow God in His own House.

CONFOUND THEIR LANGUAGE

Since the plot of the enemy was possible because of the power and focus of their unified language, God decided to disrupt it by confounding their language. That is where we get the name *babel*. *Confound* is the Hebrew word *balal* meaning *to fodder, to overflow (specifically with oil), to mix; - anoint,* and *mingle*.[7] The same word is translated *mingle*, thirty-seven times. How did God confound their language? He mingled and overflowed it with oil. In other words, language came from God and is made possible by the oil of His Spirit. How do I know this? It was the Holy Ghost on the Day of Pentecost, Who empowered the Believers with the gift of new tongues. Man was empowered with the gift of speech when God breathed into man His Spirit. The God who created language has the ability to mingle it.

GATES OF THE GODS

Babel means *"gate of baal or gate of the gods."* There was so much demonic activity through the occult and false religions created by demons, that the people of that generation were able to access gates, portals, and doors to the unseen. They had access to the supernatural realm illegally, through the occult. Some of what we call technology over the years was actually the results of accessing one of these "evil gates." The reason God destroyed all living creatures on the Earth in Noah's flood was because of this. We do not realize how advanced that generation was. They were more advanced than we are currently. They accessed electricity. They had vehicles, telecommunications, automation, and industrial science. The great pyramid that was erected during their generation still cannot be duplicated today with all of our power equipment and technology. I am reminded of the movie *Star Wars*. The people appeared to be very primitive, but their technology was sophisticated and futuristic.

God had to destroy that generation because they did not properly progress to levels of information they had, because it was illegally given to man by the fallen angels of Genesis chapter six who married human women and produced the diabolical hybrid race called "Nephilim." These fallen angels and their reprobate seed of giants introduced to mankind forbidden things like sorcery, witchcraft, the black arts, divination, and pharmaceuticals. The word *sorcery* is the Greek word *pharmakeia*. Strong's Concordance of the Bible defines *pharmakeia* as *the use of medicine, drugs, or spells*. The fallen angels and their wicked seed of giants ushered mankind into the sinister season of forbidden technology and witchcraft that we have not seen since. The giants, themselves, were hybrids and they mixed everything in creation in order to create evil creatures. This is where vampires, werewolves, minotaurs, mermaids, and even dinosaurs came from. They did not just introduce man to advanced levels of technology, but did it from evil, occultic dimensions that made it forbidden and treacherous. Genesis 6:5 says:

And God saw that the of man was great in the earth, and that every imagination of the thoughts of his heart was only evil continually. wickedness

THE SERPENT & THE CROSS

Humans are born in sin and possess a sin nature since the fall of man in the Garden of Eden. However, even in this state, we were still salvageable to God. The tampering of human DNA and the mixing of the rest of creation is what caused the world to come to an end. The mixing of human and angelic DNA is prohibited. God did not create these Nephilim, and there would be no deliverance for their race. These fallen angels and their diabolical seed did more than mix the DNA of angels and humans. Through the darkest of evil practices they began to mix all of creation to the point that the Scriptures record this in Genesis 6:12:

And God looked upon the earth, and behold, it was corrupt; for all flesh had corrupted his way upon the earth.

This was not from the normal progression of sin in man. But this records the results from evil, supernatural interference from these fallen angels. These fallen angels and their sons who are called "demi-gods" in mythology were worshipped by mankind. They possessed supreme knowledge and supernatural powers. God did not want the wicked technology (sorcery), hybrid creatures, and fallen world of that day to endure, and this was the purpose of the Flood. He literally cleansed the Earth from the filth of the forbidden practices of that age and chose not to include the details of how advanced the civilization was and how they accessed the technology.

Unfortunately, the more civilization advances technologically, sin increases exponentially. It happened in Noah's day, and it is repeating itself today as knowledge is increasing. Before the invention of different forms of transportation (buggies, trains, cars, and airplanes) mankind could sin, but was limited to who, what, when, where, and how. Transportation escalated our ability to break laws. Multiply this truth by a million and we have the results of the internet. It made the world a lot smaller and has given us access to anywhere in the world, at any time. The access and availability to every kind of evil imaginable is at the fingertips of anyone with a smartphone. The invention of the Babylonish internet is a gate of the gods to reintroduce mankind to the forbidden knowledge and acts that were judged and destroyed in the Flood.

V

PYTHON PLAN-DEMIC

If there has ever been a time in history where the serpent's hissing, whispers of cunningness, and divination of words has cast a spell on the minds of the entire world, it is today. We have literally witnessed with our own eyes and ears; the entire world fall sway to the serpent's forked tongue as billions allowed themselves to be inoculated with satan's fear. The Covid-19 pandemic is more of a "plan-demic." Without any real force, billions of people willfully gave up their rights and abandoned all common sense because of fear of a virus that is not any deadlier than the annual influenza. The serpent used his divination over all nations and people groups with the unleashing of this virus. Not one shot was fired in order to get the masses on every continent to buckle in fear and comply with the overreaching dictates of evil governments. Because of fear, all the powers that be had to do was to mandate their will on the people. The serpent hissed and we automatically abandoned our businesses and jobs. The serpent whispered and every nation locked down. The serpent told us who was essential and who was not. The serpent instructed us that big box stores were essential and small businesses were not. This resulted in companies like Amazon literally doubling their wealth in this season. The serpent determined that weed dispensaries, abortion clinics, and liquor stores were essential during a pandemic while demanding every church, mosque, temple, and synagogue to close their doors. It is one thing for these things to be mandated, but it is another thing for the people to comply so easily, especially in countries that are free. Because of the fear of a virus, the masses gave up many freedoms and liberties they possessed. This worked like a charm and now that the serpent knows how easy it is to get the entire world to march to his beat, he will never let this control go.

On February 6, 2023, Batya Ungar-Sargon aired a video on *The Hill* titled *How Elites EXPLOITED The Pandemic To STEAL From The Middle Class*:

"We all know now about the epic flip-flops of those who anointed themselves representatives of 'the science,' and how they pushed lockdowns, the vaccines, and vaccine mandates, legislating their own preferences, regardless of the consent of the governed. From the safety of their own homes, which skyrocketed in value, 'leftist elites' and medical, political, journalistic and policy fields imposed what worked for them. Indeed, what made them even richer were the millions of working-class Americans, whose labor they relied on to survive. One in five small businesses closed down, while Fortune 500 companies saw record sales. Private school children soared astronomically ahead of their public-school counterparts, who were relegated to *Zoom* learning by the 'laptop classes regime,' even those with no access to a computer. The pandemic was not just responsible for the deaths of millions of Americans, it turns out, it was also the largest transfer of wealth from the middle and working classes to the credentialed elite and billionaire classes, who cast anyone who opposed lockdowns as moral perverts, while they watched their own bank accounts swell. Then, when it came time to end the lockdowns, they demanded that you take the vaccine to protect them, while you serve them, so they could feel comfortable being waited on by you in restaurants and hospitals. From the start the pandemic pitted the interest of middle- and working-class Americans against those of the elites. A largely white collar, knowledge industry email cast was easily able to start working from home. But rather than recognize the economic privilege of getting to stay home making banana bread and buying Peloton bikes, the 'pajama class' dressed this privilege up as virtue, which correlated strongly with the lingering terror around getting Covid. It was a terror that working class Americans: Amazon delivery drivers, grocery store stockers, truckers, and police officers, simply could not afford. They had to continue to work throughout the worst of the pandemic, delivering food and safety to members of the 'liberal elite' and sconced in their homes denounced anyone who opposed the draconian lockdown measures of blue states as a 'grandma killer.' In other words, while relying on the labor of the working class, an over-credentialed elite demanded that the gap between the 'unwashed' exposed masses and the safely protected rich, grow even wider. They demanded endless lockdo.wns that didn't slow the spread of Covid, though they did grow the gap separating the elites' children from the Black and Hispanic kids whose schools were forced to close over and over by the teachers' union. As the lockdowns reduced millions of small business owners to poverty and swelled the stocks of big box megastore stocks, the elites brayed for more. Their 'boredom shopping sprees' gave Amazon record profits while middle class business owners, with their savings gone, and their businesses dead, committed suicide. And throughout, liberal elites somehow convinced themselves that they were the 'good guys,' the ones who 'cared about the collective' as opposed to those evil individualists who refused to see their life savings go up in smoke without a complaint, or who were worried about what a brand new vaccine might do to their teenage sons.[1]

If everyone on the planet took the Covid-19 vaccine, we still would not get to herd immunity for the simple fact that the vaccine does not work. We were sold the greatest lie in human history next to what the serpent told Eve at the tree of the knowledge of good and evil.

WORLD HEALTH ⊕RGANIZATION

Globally, as of 5:37pm CET, 22 November 2022, there have been 635,229,101 confirmed cases of COVID-19, including 6,602,552 deaths, reported to the World Health Organization or World Homicide Organization. As of November 16, 2022, a total of 12,943,741,540 vaccine doses have been administered. [2]

- In May 2021, the World Health Organization said that the COVID-19 Vaccination will give you 95% protection against COVID-19.
- In June 2021, the World Health Organization said that the COVID-19 Vaccination will give you 70% protection against COVID-19.
- In July 2021, the World Health Organization said that the COVID-19 Vaccination will give you 50% protection against COVID-19.
- In August 2021, the World Health Organization said that the COVID-19 vaccination will not give you protection against COVID-19. However, it reduces the spread of COVID-19.

- In September 2021, the World Health Organization said that the COVID-19 vaccination will not give you protection against COVID-19 and it will not reduce the spread of COVID-19. However, it will reduce the severity of COVID-19 should you contract it.

- In October 2021, the World Health Organization said that the COVID-19 vaccination will not give you protection against COVID-19 and it will not reduce the spread of COVID-19. In addition, it will not reduce the severity of COVID-19 should you contract it. However, it will reduce the hospitalizations from COVID-19.

- In November 2021, the World Health Organization said that the COVID-19 vaccination will not give you protection against COVID-19 and it will not reduce the spread of COVID-19. In addition, it will not reduce the severity of COVID-19 or reduce the hospitalizations from COVID-19. However, you will not die from COVID-19 if you take the vaccine.

- In December 2021, the World Health Organization said that the COVID-19 vaccination will not give you protection against COVID-19 and it will not reduce the spread of COVID-19. In addition, it will not reduce the severity of COVID-19 or reduce the hospitalizations from COVID-19. In fact, one may die from COVID-19, even if they took the COVID-19 vaccination.[3]

DECEPTION IN DEATH

A very revealing and powerful book exposing the lies and deception of this "plan-demic" and vaccine is written by Dr. Karina Reiss and Dr. Sucharit Bhakdi titled *Corona False Alarm? Facts and Figures.* In an interview on the podcast *Financial Rebellion with Catherine Austin Fitts,* Dr. Bhakdi states:

"You can't get something injected into your muscles and have antibodies made against them that is going to be released into the bloodstream and expect that these antibodies are going to stop a virus from entering the lung cells from the air. It was clear from the very beginning that this vaccination was going to fail. It couldn't work, never could've worked, and will never work. It became clear that this so-called vaccine did not protect against this infection at all. Zero. Thus, there could be no benefit. There had never been any benefit. The data showing benefit was fraudulent from the first go. This told the world that the whole business was a hoax. This hoax was revealed formally at the end of 2021. The second thing that became noticeably clear was that not only was there no benefit, but the risk was absolutely horrendous. So, we're looking at a risk-benefit ratio that is infinite. (There is) no benefit and (there is) risk without end."[4]

That was a clear indication that this whole nonsense had to be stopped. However, it was not stopped. This made it clear to everyone in the world who had any common sense that something very criminal was on the way. It was born of intent and deliberation. It became clear that this vaccine was harming and killing people and what we were (and are) looking at, is genocide. Anyone with any sense of humanity would say straight up that the Federal Drug Administration (FDA), Center for Disease Control (CDC), National Institute of Health (NIH), all the health authorities in the world, and all the politicians in the world, even if they had any blind intent in the beginning, it was their duty to stop this.

However, it hasn't stopped. And this is something that is so horrifying because they are destroying lives. Think about the way they're destroying the existence of people. They are taking away their material existence. The global populist is getting poorer. Money is being taken away from them. The taxes that people pay aren't being used to treat them, but to pay for these poisons that are killing them.

The following evidence came out as decisive proof that these vaccines were killing people. Ana Bokad, a retired professor, and his team examined the tissues of individuals who died of the Covid-19 vaccine. He found a pattern: they all died following their vaccinations. They were ages 28 to 90 years old. All of them died after vaccination, but their deaths were not attributed (officially) at all to the vaccinations. Half of them died at home, in the car, or at work. They died suddenly, without any apparent cause, and only two had been in the ICU because of another ailment. What he found was that respective of age, sex, and true cause of death, the same findings were made in these individuals' organs. Pathological changes were found in ninety percent of the hearts he examined and eighty percent of the lungs. These findings occurred in both the lungs and hearts of the individuals, and this, of course, never happens. These changes were typical of "auto-attack," meaning the new system was attacking the individual. The changes were inflammation of the vessels (mainly small vessels) and the organs. Lymphocytes were entering the vessel walls and the organs. This pattern doesn't occur in any other disease that is known.[5]

The conclusive proof that these vaccines were killing people was found when Bokad and his team discovered that the spike proteins could be detected at these sites. The spike proteins had either been produced at these sites or travelled to these sites in the vaccinated people. This was also discovered in other labs. First of all, the lifetime of these gene-based agents was horribly long. As a result, the gene of the spike proteins were found to be active in the lymph nodes of vaccinated individuals sixty days after vaccination. What a horrible thought! Secondly, the spike itself was found to be present in the circulation of people who had been vaccinated for weeks. This means the spike had been produced over an extended period of time. The last horrifying discovery was made that the RNA of the virus that is taken out by a cell is very rapidly reversed and transcribed into the DNA in the nucleus within six hours. This opens the door so that the gene of the virus can be inserted into the individual's genome.[6] Everyone still upholding this vaccine program must be taken to court!

FREEDOM OF INFORMATION

The United Kingdom requested the use of the Freedom of Information Act concerning Covid-19. Therefore, information from March 13, 2020, to January 7, 2022, regarding the vaccine was released. This information included a total of 127,704 recorded deaths from Covid-19 within that time period. Total deaths within 28 days of a positive test were 152,872. Deaths where Covid-19 is mentioned on the death certificate was 174,233. However, the Freedom of Information Act request revealed a fourth figure. Deaths from Covid-19 with no other underlying causes were only 17,101.[7] In other words, people who had no heart disease, no diabetes, no lung disease, and no other ailments but were completely healthy, died of Covid-19.

Deaths due to Covid-19 with no pre-existing conditions in England and Wales: For the year 2020, there was a total of 9,400 deaths.[8] In 2020, deaths from the age of 0-64 were 1,549, and age 65+ were 7,851. The average age of these figures combined together was 81.5 years old. The vast majority of the deaths involved much older people.[9] The first quarter (January - March) of 2021, total deaths from Covid-19 was 6,483. Age 0 to 64 were 1,560 deaths and age 65 and over were 4,923 total deaths. The average age of death from the combined was 81.5 years old. The second quarter (April – June) of 2021, total deaths were 346. Age 0 to 64 were 153, and age 65 and up were 193 deaths.[10] The third quarter (July – September) of 2021, total deaths were 1,142. Age 0 to 64 were 512, and age 65 and up were 630 deaths. Therefore, the year 2020 and the first three quarters of 2021, total deaths from Covid-19 alone (the only attributed cause) was 17,371. Of this number 13,597 were 65 or over. Only 3,774 were under 65. Therefore, the average age of death in the United Kingdom from Covid-19 in this period was 82.5 years.[11] The average life expectancy in the United Kingdom from 2018 to 2020 is 79 years old for males and 82.9 years old for females. This indicates that the average age of death from Covid-

19 was actually greater than the average life expectancy in the United Kingdom.[12]

UNMASK

If the overwhelmingly most detrimental age during this plan-demic was 81 years old, why in the world did everyone need to lockdown, socially distance, sacrifice their businesses, careers, jobs, and stay home from school? Daily, while the Democrats were screaming, "Follow the science," we did not know they meant political science. The serpent weaponized the "plan-demic" like no other time in history. Before Covid-19 was unleashed on the earth, most people understood that masks did not actually protect you from a virus. I have friends who are doctors and nurses and they told me that they learned about the inadequacies of masks in medical school. They told me that Professors used certain experiments to show how even N-95 masks did not completely prevent the entrance of a virus. On February 29, 2021, the U.S. surgeon general tweeted: "Seriously people – STOP BUYING MASKS… They are NOT effective in preventing (the) general public from catching #Coronavirus."[13] We are living in a season where the serpent has brainwashed the masses to the point where they do not even believe what they see with their own eyes and hear with their own ears. I have shown people the words on the very box of masks that they purchased and how it clearly states that the mask does not prevent the spread of corona viruses. After reading the words from the actual manufacturer, they would look at me with a glare that seemed to indicate that I was a conspiracy theorist and denier of truth. What do you do with that?

CONVALESCENT CRIME

Around the country, we witnessed a massive number of elderly deaths. This "plan-demic" season has been a season of multiplied elderly murders. Very early on in the "plan-demic," the government and powers that be knew that the 65+ age group was the group at greatest risk.[14] Predominantly, these elderly people counted for most of the Covid-19 deaths. Yet the government and authorities, kept pushing fear and control on everyone. I call it murder because of places like New York, where reprobate ex-Governor Cuomo signed an executive order to make all seniors who had been diagnosed with Covid-19 return to the convalescent homes where they ended up infecting others in these elderly homes.[15] Thousands of our precious elderly died from the intentional lunacy of evil political leaders like Cuomo. To make matters worse, protocol during this season dictated that family and friends could not physically visit those infected with Covid-19 who were in the care of the hospital or medical facility. Due to fear and ignorance, thousands of our precious elderly loved ones died alone, afraid, and without hope. Deprived of human touch, love, personal prayers, and interaction, I cannot imagine the level of trauma and abandonment this must have been for our elderly. We are going to look back at this season of insanity and cringe at the level of stupidity and lunacy our world fell victim to. More importantly, we will remember how it was all accomplished from the simple yet profound power of the tongue. The serpent's henchmen did not shoot a bullet, muster the military, or really use any form of force to accomplish his worldwide shutdown of freedom. He simply used the power of words. The serpent used his mouthpiece in media, government, and social media to change the world as we knew it, in a day. The President simply asked for two weeks to curb the virus.[16] The governors simply spoke the need for mandates. The mayors simply requested the Churches to close their doors. The Centers for Disease Control and Prevention (CDC) calmly asked the people to wear masks.[17] Now look where we are today. The enemy understands the power of words better than God's own people. Our Lord is called the Word of God and we still do not properly comprehend the essence of this ability.

The craftiness of the serpent's tongue had the entire world on lockdown, socially distancing, wearing masks, and paralyzed in fear about a virus that was literally no deadlier than the annual flu. Our children were forced to stay home from school and be subject to remote learning and that turned out to be an absolute disaster![18] During this same "plan-demic" season, there has been a great increase in domestic violence, hunger, and suicide.[19] Statistics are currently coming out that show the major cause of death during the "plan-demic" season came from the neglect and lack of care for people with serious conditions like cancer, diabetes, and those who were in need of major surgeries.[20] Since healthcare providers stopped treating everything that was not Covid-19, there has been a terrible loss of life and that was 100% avoidable. The cure was definitely worse than the disease! It all began with our government asking the people to sacrifice two weeks to help curb the spread of the disease. That was in the very beginning. Two and a half years later, they still requested egregious mandates that suppressed our lives and liberties. If we let the devil ride, he is going to want to drive. Freedom is not something to be trifled with and this can be seen, clearly, in the Garden of Eden at the Tree of the Knowledge of Good and Evil.

Hydroxychloroquine

What would you call someone who intentionally suppresses the distribution of and even labels people "conspiracy theorists," when they communicate about a drug that could save thousands from death due to a virus? Most would say that person or persons are indeed "cold-blooded murderers." Well, this is exactly what the Democratic Party and its political hacks in the media, CDC, and big tech companies did. They suppressed the information flow, attacked people personally, and even canceled anyone who openly spoke about the positive results of the very inexpensive drug, hydroxychloroquine. The very hypocrites who were yelling "listen to the science," ignored the science every step of the way during this "plan-demic." They did not care about your education, expertise in the medical field, or how distinguished your career was. If you disagreed with their diabolical scheme, you were openly labeled "a denier of science" and "a conspiracy theorist." The Frontline Doctors of America spoke against the lies that the government and the CDC were telling the American people. Consequently, these Frontline Doctors were swiftly discounted and censored on all social media platforms.[21] After President Trump openly suggested that hydroxychloroquine could be a viable treatment for Covid-19 (as a group of doctors sat with him, who gave him this information), the Democrats and mainstream media had a complete meltdown and spent the next few weeks calling him everything from "a peddler of snake oil," to "a buffoon," "worse than Hitler," and "President of death." From the beginning of the "plan-demic" until Trump left the office, the false prophets of baal in the mainstream media accused Trump of being responsible for every single death from Covid-19, and daily kept a count of the deaths, placing the count next to his name on the news. While at the same time, the mainstream media absolutely canceled anyone who suggested the use of hydroxychloroquine. They knew the drug had positive results and did not care. At the time of their outrage over the mention of the drug, nothing else was actually working. What did they have to lose? Saving lives is what they did not want. They led with the purpose of saving lives in all the deception and overreach, but it was never about saving lives. If the leaders of the Democratic Party really desired to save lives and stop the spread of the virus, they would not have allowed our southern border to continue to be wide open. If they were really concerned about eliminating the spread of the virus, anyone coming through the southern border would be tested for the virus and made to take the vaccine. However, neither of these things ever happened and still are not happening. They don't care about illegal aliens crossing into America by the millions unvaccinated and able to spread the virus. On the other hand, we are American citizens with rights, and they demanded that we be vaccinated. In one breath, these "double-standard Democrats" are screaming "my body, my choice," when it comes to having the right to murder their own babies in the womb, but when it comes to free citizens refusing to inject a foreign substance into their bodies, they yelled how those people were "deniers of science." Joe Biden actually opened his mouth and let the forked tongue loose. He stated that the unvaccinated are "the new pandemic." If you didn't realize satan was working through this shell of a man, then you never will.

The cruel and heartless Governor Andrew M. Cuomo of New York used his bully pulpit to stop the distribution of prescriptions for hydroxychloroquine in his state. All the while, he sent all infected elderly back into the convalescent homes to infect those who were healthy. Doctors knew of the positive treatment of hydroxychloroquine and attempted to prescribe it for their elderly patients and the pharmacists in New York refused to fill the prescriptions. This was no less than murder by neglect. Throughout the years, the Democratic Party is "a party of murder." The Democratic Party promoted slavery, Jim Crow Laws, segregation, abortion, and now Covid-19 mandates and so-called "protocols."[22] Literally thousands could have potentially been saved by a drug that has been approved by the Federal Drug Administration (FDA) for decades and hydroxychloroquine is very inexpensive to purchase and useful for the treatment of Covid-19.[23] However, the "Democratic machine" who controls every major industry in America said, "NO!" As a result, thousands died in America for absolutely no reason besides the sheer arrogance and murderous spirit of the Democrats. All the while, daily, they blamed Trump for every life that was lost from the virus. However, when Biden became president, in his first year, more people died of Covid than the previous year under Trump, not one major network attributed their deaths to Biden. This is the power of the serpent's tongue in American politics.

Once the serpent's lies and fears take root in the hearts of the masses, it is exceedingly difficult to uproot. If Hitler had Google, Facebook, Twitter, and Amazon, he would have taken over the world. His sinister plan was short-circuited by the lack of technology. Have you noticed during this "plan-demic" that one of the greatest strategies of the serpent was to label anyone who disagreed with, challenged, or presented opposing opinions to the lies, misinformation, and disinformation, as "conspiracy theorists," "racists," and/or "purveyors of misinformation"? The serpent is using the

Democratic Party, intelligence agencies, big tech giants, the mainstream media, the educational system, and the healthcare system as his base to monopolize the flow of information. This, along with Artificial Intelligence (AI) technology, leave most people absolutely clueless as to the profound affect that social media platforms have on them. In addition, "Big Brother" and others are unlawfully accumulating your personal information. After Donald J. Trump won the 2016 Presidential Election, *Google* admitted they underestimated him and the populist movement, and vowed they would use the unlimited power of their company to make sure it did not happen again. Guess what? They did exactly that. *Google* used their influence against Donald J. Trump in the 2020 Elections.[24] *Google* openly admitted that they had the power to alter American politics. This power comes directly from that old serpent.

When you tune into *CNN, MSNBC, ABC, and CBS News*, you are listening to the serpent's forked tongue. When you log onto *Facebook, Twitter, Instagram,* and/or *TikTok* you are being seduced by the serpent's tongue. What you do not know can hurt you. The Artificial Intelligence technology of these platforms are amazing. Many of the creators of these platforms do not allow their children to utilize them because they know the control it has and damage it does.[25]

REMDESIVIR

During the pandemic, when the sick went to the hospitals in Hawai'i (as well as other Democratic run states), the hospitals were pushing a drug called *Remdesivir*. The first study on this drug was tested in four regions and it was pulled after six months because it killed 54% of the users. In February 2020, China was seeking a patent on *Remdesivir*.[26]

The second study on *Remdesivir* was in early March 2020 and it was tested on subjects in Japan, United States, and Canada. After being on *Remdesivir* for only five days, 8% of the users had to be taken off of *Remdesivir* because they were dying, 23% had serious adverse effects (multiple organs shut down and other side effects), and 31% had acute kidney failure.[27]

One of the studies on Remdesivir showed a 54% mortality rate. Yet this is the drug that they are treating your loved ones with, in the hospitals as part of their "Covid protocol." Dr. Anthony Fauci pushed the use of *Remdesivir* in the hospitals and said that it would help people. So why the push for *Remdesivir*? *Remdesivir* makes Covid-19 look more deadly than it really is! *Remdesivir* allows the lungs and other parts of the body to be filled with water. Then, when the lungs are filled with water, the patients have a tough time breathing and the healthcare professionals will say that the patients cannot breathe due to Covid-19. In many hospitals around America, giving the patient *Remdesivir* was part of their "Covid-19 protocol." Fauci, who knew the results of the *Remdesivir* studies knew what would happen when a patient took *Remdesivir,* and he tried to blame it on Covid-19. The supposed surge in Covid-19 cases resulting in death in 2021 in America was due to patients being treated with *Remdesivir.*[28]

Margaret's Testimony

A member of my church became ill during the pandemic, and this is her eyewitness account of how the hospital tried desperately to get her to take Remdesivir.

"When I went to the hospital with pneumonia, I had firsthand experience with a doctor and two nurses who tried to give me *Remdesivir,* even though my first two Covid tests in the emergency room were negative. Also, I personally know five people in Hawai'i who have died from taking this deadly drug given to each of them in different hospitals here in Hawai'i, on the Island of Oahu, and on the Island of Kauai.

In September 2021, I went to the hospital because I was dehydrated, and my oxygen saturation level was down to 84. In the emergency room, I was diagnosed with pneumonia. I was tested for Covid-19 twice in the emergency room and both times, it was negative. About five hours later, they put me on the 'Covid Floor' in the hospital. When I asked the hospital staff why I was on the 'Covid Floor,' they said that I had 'Covid symptoms.' The nurse who checked me into the hospital room prepped me for what she said, 'is going to happen to me.' She told me that I would have to wear some device on both legs for circulation 'so that I wouldn't get blood clots,' and she told me that I would 'be on a CPap (or BPap)' and then 'end up on a ventilator.' When the nurse left the room, I said aloud, 'I rebuke that in Jesus' Name!'

After I was checked into the hospital room, another nurse did a third Covid Test on me. In my opinion, the hospital was determined to get a positive test result, no matter what. I told the nurse that administered the test that I was already tested twice and both times it was negative. However, she continued to do the Covid Test. I believe that the hospital was determined to diagnose me with Covid-19, even though they already told me that I had pneumonia in the emergency room. Later, after I was released, I found out that hospitals in Hawai'i receive $301,000 for every patient diagnosed with Covid-19.[29] This money comes from the U.S. Department of Health and Human Services' (HHS) $30 billion 'Emergency Fund' and is designated for hospitals according to the *Coronavirus Aid, Relief, and Economic Security Act*.[30]

The doctor who came into my room one day said that they were going to give me *Remdesivir*. At the time, I could not remember exactly why I should not take it, but I knew that I was NOT to take *Remdesivir*. When the doctor asked me why I wouldn't take it, I told her that I believed that 'the drug came from aborted fetal tissues.' I could not remember what I read about *Remdesivir* and got it mixed up with *Regeneron* (monoclonal anti-bodies), a few times. *Regeneron* was developed from aborted fetal tissues.[31] After the doctor left the room, a nurse came in and was extremely aggressive. She told me that she treated Covid-19 in many hospitals around the country. She worked in Texas, Florida, California, and a few other places before coming to work in Hawai'i to pay off her student loans. This nurse was very adamant about me taking *Remdesivir*. She said that *Remdesivir* was part of the 'Covid 19 protocol' in the hospitals. The way she pushed the drug one would think she was getting a bonus or commission for every patient that takes *Remdesivir*. I was not going to be one of those patients.

Shortly thereafter, a second nurse came into my room and tried to get me to take *Remdesivir*. I refused the drug, and I strongly believe that if I took *Remdesivir*, I would not be alive today. The next day, they moved me to another room because initially I was in an ICU room on the 'Covid Floor.' Then, on the third or fourth day, they moved me to the other side of the hospital. Finally, they moved me out of the Covid-19 patient area. Yay! I was in the hospital for a total of five days and was released on Tuesday, the day after Labor Day in September 2021.

When I was discharged from the hospital, the doctor sent me home with a prescription for *Dexamethasone.* Like *Remdesivir*, *Dexamethasone* also shuts down the kidneys but in lower numbers (in up to 4% of its users).[32]

This was a terrible experience to have to go through, especially since they would not allow me to have visitors when I was in the hospital. My only connection to the outside world was through my cell phone that I kept charged. When I returned home, I found out that two of my friends, both Born Again Believers died in the hospital. Both of them took *Remdesivir*. One of the women was warned beforehand not to take *Remdesivir* by a brother in the Lord. However, she told the person who warned her over the phone that she 'trusted the doctors and the hospital staff.'

Shortly after that, two more of my friends (one man and one woman), both Born Again Believers, went into the hospital, were diagnosed with Covid-19, were treated with *Remdesivir*, and went on ventilators. Before the Man of God went into the hospital, he told his family that he did NOT want to be put on a ventilator. However, for whatever reason, the family consented to put him on a ventilator, despite his request. Within one hour of being on that ventilator, he passed away.

Then in January 2022, a pastor friend of mine on Kauai was also admitted into the hospital for Covid-19. They treated her with *Remdesivir*. I am not sure if she went on a ventilator, but I know that she passed away, too. That's five of my friends in Hawaii who died, in my opinion, due to being 'treated' with *Remdesivir*.

I was told that seven pastors on Kauai died in the hospital of Covid-19, in 2021. Seven is a substantial number since the population on Kauai is exceedingly small. All of these pastors were given *Remdesivir*, the so-called 'Covid 19 protocol.'

While I am grateful to be alive so that I can tell others about the Gospel of the Kingdom, I am angry and saddened about the unnecessary deaths that occurred due to the effects of *Remdesivir*. This so-called 'Covid-19 treatment' should never have been given to patients. *Remdesivir* killed many innocent people in Hawaii."

VI

FOX SNAKE FAUCI

Every wise student of the Bible understands the scholarly importance of looking up the meaning of names. The fact that God gave Adam the responsibility and privilege of naming all the animals in Creation speaks to the awesome authority He delegated to His first man because whatever you name, you impose its name and nature. Adam not only named the serpent but in part composed the serpent's cunning craftiness. One of the major personalities during the "plandemic" season was Dr. Anthony Stephen Fauci. A look into the meaning of his name will speak volumes to the actual role he played in this menacing timetable.

Anthony comes from the Roman family name *Antonius*. Some say it means *priceless one* or *highly praiseworthy*. *Stephen* is a common variant of *Steven* and is derived from the Greek *Stephanos* meaning *wreath, crown, and by extension reward, honor, renown, fame, from the verb (Stephein), to encircle, and to wreath.* Fauci is an Italian surname. It is derived from the Sicilian word for *sickle* and originated as an occupational surname referring metonymically to *makers of sickles.*[1] So, let's put his full name together and see what we find. He who is highly praiseworthy, and the priceless one, wearing a crown, or wreath of honor, and whose fame is as the sickle maker. If you were not around during the AIDS epidemic, you may not know of Dr. Fauci's insidious activities and horrible mistakes. Somehow, he became the face during this "plan-demic." Dr. Fauci was uplifted as the paramount authority on all things pertaining to the virus. The mainstream media propped him up as highly praiseworthy and priceless. He could do or say nothing wrong, no matter how many times he changed his opinion. His opinion changed so often that he inherited the nickname, "Flip-Flop Fauci." He initially told Americans that wearing a mask was only for their "own emotional security" and that "it did not give any protection from the virus." After that statement by Fauci, the Democratic left came after him and he immediately flipped. Then, he came out saying that he made that statement because there was "a shortage of masks," and he did not want the public to rush to buy the masks when "the frontline healthcare workers needed them more." Fauci lied and continues to lie because the powers that be tell him to. The serpent's tongue will lie on a dime and change it as needed, in order to keep the masses deceived.

Corona means crown and refers to the appearance that the corona virus gets from the spike proteins sticking out of them. The alcoholic beverage Corona bears a crown as its logo on the product. It is not a coincidence that the names Anthony and Corona mean crown. Dr. Fauci is wearing the crown that comes from the Corona crown because he directly financed Gain of Function Research in Wuhan, China where the virus began. The pathological lies from these people remind me of a conversation I overheard among a group of men. One man asked the other men in the group, "How do you respond when you are caught red-handed in a lie?" The other men instantly replied in unison, "Never admit the truth." In other words, just stick to your story, no matter how much proof is presented regarding your guilt. Lie, lie, lie! This is a picture of the Democratic Party and all the powerful players during this "plan-demic." Dr. Fauci has been brought before the Senate Oversight Committee a few times now, and proof of his direct involvement with funding Wuhan's Gain of Function Research has been presented before the committee.[2] How does Dr. Fauci respond? He simply continues to lie with a straight face. The serpent's tongue is only built one way: one tongue with two endings (mix a little of the truth with a lot of the lie).

Sickle Maker

The name *Fauci* means *sickle maker*. His role during the "plan-demic" is very prophetic. The word *sickle* is a noun and means: *An agricultural implement consisting of a curved metal blade with a short handle fitted on a tang.*[3] Let's examine what the Scriptures say about the sickle.

Put ye in the sickle, for the harvest is ripe: come, get you down; for the press is full, the fats overflow; for their wickedness is great.
Joel 3:13

Revelation 14:14-19 reads:

And I looked, and behold a white cloud, and upon the cloud one sat like unto the Son of man, having on his head a golden crown, and in his hand a sharp sickle.

And another angel came out of the temple, crying with a loud voice to him that sat on the cloud, Thrust in thy sickle, and reap: for the time is come for thee to reap; for the harvest of the earth is ripe.

And he that sat on the cloud thrust in his sickle on the earth; and the earth was reaped.

And another angel came out of the temple which is in heaven, he also having a sharp sickle.

And another angel came out from the altar, which had power over fire; and cried with a loud cry to him that had the sharp sickle, saying, Thrust in thy sharp sickle, and gather the clusters of the vine of the earth; for her grapes are fully ripe.

And the angel thrust in his sickle into the earth, and gathered the vine of the earth, and cast it into the great winepress of the wrath of God.

In the Book of Revelation, Jesus is seen wearing a golden crown, and in his hand is a sharp sickle. Is this a coincidence? No. The One who wears the crown is the One who reaps the harvest. We know the devil is never the originator, he is just an imitator. The name *Anthony Stephen Fauci* means *priceless one, highly praiseworthy who wears the crown (fame, reward, and honor) and is the sickle maker.*[4] Dr. Fauci is one of the serpent's frauds. Jesus is the Only Priceless One Who deserves the highest praise. He's not only the King of kings and wears the Golden Crown of Majesty, but we cast our crowns down before Him. Since He gave His life for us, and rose again for our justification, He is the true Sickle Maker, and is worthy to put in His sickle because the harvest is ripe and the winepress is full, because the world's wickedness is great.

In the end, the Lord will be the One wearing a golden crown and sticking His sickle in the Earth to reap a harvest of the wicked ones. However, in this "plan-demic" season, the serpent has elevated Dr. Fauci as the one who is praiseworthy, the one who wears the crown, and is the sickle maker. As we noticed in Scripture, the sickle is used for reaping harvests. That harvest can be good or evil. The harvest of souls being reaped in the "plan-demic" is from an evil worldwide agenda. Fauci is directly connected to the very lab in Wuhan, China where the virus was unleashed on the world.[5] Fauci funded this lab's Gain of Function Research where they were intentionally altering the virus (that is only naturally found among beasts) to be able to penetrate human cells and infect man. Fauci then becomes the face and authority over the "plan-demic." If this isn't "the fox guarding the chickencoop," I don't know what is. Fauci knows the whole truth concerning this outbreak better than anyone else and he has not been held accountable in the least. As the death toll rose during the "plan-demic," the "sickle maker" was the very one behind it. He knows masks have no protection against a virus and said that in the beginning. However, soon after, Fauci has lied every step of the way. He knows we are supposed to quarantine the sick, not the healthy, but he still approved quarantines. The evil, corrupt powers that be, have propped up Fauci and made him "the priceless one who wears the crown." Nevertheless, very soon his day of reckoning is coming, and he will give an account for every innocent soul who was infected and died from his "mad science," and pompous agenda. The "sickle maker" will soon bust hell wide open and realize he never wore a crown. The sickle is what the Grim Reaper holds, and the sickle and hammer is the symbol of Communism.

Facts about Fauci

There were seven facts Dr. Fauci knew from the beginning of the "plan-demic":

1. He knew American tax dollars went to Eco Health and that money was funneled to a lab in Wuhan, China.

2. He knew Eco Health was given an exemption from the pause on Gain of Function research.

3. The security standards at this lab in Wuhan, China was deficient.

4. Dr. Fauci knew that Eco Health was not in compliance with their grant reporting requirements.

5. Gain of Function was, in fact, being conducted in the lab in Wuhan, China.

6. The P3CO Interagency review process was not followed in approving the grant to Eco Health.

7. Dr. Fauci knew that the Covid-19 virus came from the lab in Wuhan, China.

Dr. Fauci had this information on February 1, 2020. What did he do with this information? Did he tell the president of the United States or anyone on his staff? No. Did he tell the experts in our government? No. Did he tell his boss, Secretary Azar? No. Did he tell any directors of our health and disease agencies? No. What Dr. Fauci did, instead, he organized a conference call on February 1, 2020, at 2 pm with Mr. Collins and eleven virologists around the world. Fauci had been handing out American tax dollars to these people for years. On that call was Dr. Gary Christian Anderson who said this the day before this infamous call, "the virus looks engineered and is not consistent with evolutionary theories." Then on the day of the call he said, "I don't know how this gets done in nature, but it will be easy to do in a lab."

They all got their stories straight and three days later the very same people who said that this virus "came from a lab" changed their tune and said that anyone who thinks that is "crazy." What a dramatic change in scientific analysis and the only intervening event was the conference call that Dr. Fauci organized. Email after email has been released exposing the lies and deceit of Dr. Fauci, and yet he remained in power and the face of this man-made "plan-demic" proving that the vaccine was not made for the Covid-19 virus, but the virus was created for the vaccine.

LOCKDOWN LIES

If lockdowns and mandates failed, why are they still being pushed? Dr. Joseph Mercola was quoted in Epoch Times, in an article on March 21, 2022:

"Hundreds of studies show lockdowns failed to meaningfully reduce Covid-19 deaths, while Covid-19 shot mandates are counterproductive and harmful. Despite this, these totalitarian schemes are ongoing. Scientists, the world over, have done a deep dive into the unprecedented lockdowns and injection mandates that characterize the Covid-19 pandemic response. Over and over again, the results confirm what many instinctively knew all along – that these totalitarian schemes didn't work and may have caused more harm than good. Despite the writing on the wall, health officials and academics continue to defend the Draconian measures. It is difficult to admit wrongdoing, especially of this magnitude.

THE SERPENT & THE CROSS

'These interventions turned a manageable pandemic into a catastrophe,' said Jeffrey Tucker, Founder and President of the Brownstone Institute. Eventually, what Tucker said will become widely known.'"[6]

Public health policies that restrict movement, ban international travel, and close schools and businesses (commonly known as lockdowns), were implemented in virtually every country around the globe during the pandemic. These restrictive policies began in China, then Italy, and then spread like wildfire from there. Simulated computer models conducted by Imperial College London researchers in 2020 suggested that lockdowns would reduce the Covid-19 mortality rate by up to 98%, an estimate that had many scholars raising eyebrows, and did not come to fruition, not even close.[7] In a literature review and meta-analysis of the effects of lockdowns on Covid-19 mortality, researchers from Johns Hopkins Institute for Applied Economics, Global Health, and the Study of Business Enterprise, Lund University and the Center for Political Studies in Copenhagen, Denmark, revealed lockdowns had "little to no effect on Covid-19 mortality."[8]

Not since the days of Noah has the serpent's forked tongue cast a spell and worked divination on the minds of the masses, like it has during this global "plan-demic." However, just as it was in Daniel chapter three in Babylon, with the erection of King Nebuchadnezzar's golden image, there will be a remnant who will not comply or bow down to the sorcery of the serpent. We would rather give God the opportunity to show Himself strong and deliver us from this world's burning fiery furnace than to obey the pathological lies of the serpent's forked tongue.

PLAN-DEMIC PEDDLERS

We do not expect our elected leaders to be unblemished in seasons of national emergencies like a pandemic. However, we most certainly do not expect them to make decisions that will infringe upon our freedoms and will harm us, especially the weakest in society like children, and the elderly. To the absolute shame of many so-called leaders around the world, this is exactly what they did to their own people. This, of course, is inexcusable!

Before the roll out of the vaccines, many of the vaccine companies' presidents and spokespersons publicly declared how their vaccines would stop the transmission of the virus. Every major mainstream media outlet preached this same rhetoric, passionately and systematically, and began to ban, censor, and attack anyone who questioned it and labeled it as "fake news" or "purveyors of misinformation." One known infamous personality was Rachel Maddow of MSNBC. On December 21, 2021, she stated this on her show titled, *If You Have Been Putting Off Vaccination. The Time is Now.*

"As a personal plea from me. If you have been putting off being vaccinated, for whatever reason, don't agonize about it. Don't let anybody make you feel bad about that. Just, make a fresh decision now. Now is the time to actually go and do it. Because we really can't afford to have you to go to the hospital right now. If you're unvaccinated, you have a much higher chance of getting this newly transmissible variant we have never seen before. And it's the unvaccinated people it's going to make sick, and we really cannot afford for you to have to go to the hospital right now. Looking around the country, depending on where you live, there is a very good chance there is no room for you in the hospital right now, if you need to go. And if you can somehow get a bed because you got covid, and you got sick from it because you weren't vaccinated, if you are able to get yourself into a bed, you're going to be filling a bed that somebody else really needs."

On April 9, 2021, Rachel Maddow aired that she got the COVID-19 vaccine and she continued to peddle the fear, lies, and deception.[9] She stated:

"Here is the thing. I feel I have total clarity now that I've done it. It's not for you. You are not doing this for yourself. If you don't care that much that you, yourself are going to get covid. What do you care about? What will move you? What does tip the scales decisively in favor of you going and getting that shot that you really don't want? Is it that you really don't want to be that person that gets it and spreads it to other people? God forbid, that if you don't get vaccinated, and you unknowingly spread it to other people, those people get sick from it or die from it. Those people give it to their family members and their mom, or their dad dies from it because of you. Because you wouldn't get vaccinated. Would you live with yourself in that circumstance? If you had the choice to get

THE SERPENT & THE CROSS

vaccinated and you decided naw, I'm scared. And that decision caused somebody else, that you know, their life because they got it from you. It's not for you. If you get vaccinated, your risk of getting really sick or dying from covid yourself, that risk basically drops to zero! And that's true with all the vaccines. If you get vaccinated, yeah, you saved yourself, more importantly you have saved everybody else. So, even if you don't want to, get your vaccine so you don't ever kill anybody with covid."

Several months later, Rachel Maddow broadcast from her home announcing that her lover of twenty-one years contracted COVID-19 and was sick for the last two weeks. Rachel told us that she thought that at one point (because of the illness), her lover would die from it. Rachel had been in quarantine so that she would not cause others to be at risk. Rachel's lover was vaccinated, so based on Rachel's own words, how was she even able to get infected? And if getting infected and dying from the virus drops to "zero" why did Rachel quarantine herself? These "false prophets of baal" lie, without a conscience, and do not even possess an iota of humility to ever apologize or admit any wrongdoing. The mainstream media are the ones screaming,

"Follow the science!" However, what they really meant is, "Follow the science fiction!" There is no telling how many people who did not want to get vaccinated, went ahead and did it because they tuned in daily to these snake oil merchants of fear and false information and suppressors of real facts. Why won't anyone address the fact that our own leaders boldly informed the public that no one would get infected with covid if we took the vaccine? Or address how the media immediately changed course after vaccinated people began to contract the virus, and without blinking, publicly stated that we would not die from covid or any variants if vaccinated? That was absolutely not what they boldly guaranteed in the beginning. Just like Rachel Maddow's mammoth lies, no one called her out on it. People continued to go along with the charade. Rachel's logic totally disregarded natural immunity and jumped ahead to villainizing the unvaccinated with the guilt of murderous hands if they did not get vaccinated.

PFIZER FARSE

The European Parliament's COVID-19 Advisory Board questioned the directors at Pfizer.[10] Robert Roos, a politician, and member of the European Parliament (MEP) is also the Vice Chair of the European Conservatives and Reformists Group. He asked the following question to the directors at Pfizer:

"Was the Pfizer covid vaccine tested on stopping the transmission of the virus before it entered the market? If not, please say it clearly. If yes, are you willing to share the data with this committee? And I really want a straight answer. I'm looking forward to it. Yes or no."

Janine Small (who was standing in for Pfizer CEO Albert Bourla), is the President of International Developed Markets at Pfizer, and she answered:

"Regarding the question around whether we knew about stopping immunization before entering the market? No. We really moved at the speed of science to really understand what is taking place in the market. And from that point of view, we had to do everything at risk."

The European Parliament's COVID-19 Advisory Board posed the same question to the other vaccine manufacturers. However, they refused to answer. Pfizer admitted what all of the medical professionals knew to be true the entire time, and that is, that everyone who took these COVID-19 vaccinations were allowing themselves to be "lab rats" because the vaccine did not have enough time to properly go through its efficacy trials. To this, President Donald Trump deserves plenty of blame, also, as he pushed these vaccines through under what was called "warp speed."[11]

Pfizer finally publicly confessed they DID NOT TEST THE VACCINE ON STOPPING THE TRANSMISSION OF THE VIRUS! In other words, it was absolutely worthless and every public figure (politician, medical professional, pastor, company executive, etc.) who spewed fear and misinformation to coerce the world to willingly take this vaccine was and is an accomplice and should be ashamed. Governments unethically and illegally fired their own workforce for not taking this fake vaccine that was never tested on the actual virus. Companies in America and around the world shamefully disgraced their very own people for standing for their right to refuse to allow something into their bodies they did not agree with, and these companies arrogantly fired them. The most egregious of them all, were the healthcare companies who dismissed and disposed of their dedicated and courageous workers who put their lives on the line during the heart of the "plan-demic," and were not extended the decency to refuse a fraudulent and pirated vaccine. As an immediate result, many corporations had a shortage of workers, and this affected their ability to serve the public. I applaud everyone who stood their ground, based on their principles, under the most stressful situations. It is during these seasons when we find out what we are really made of. Pressure bursts pipes, and unfortunately, many in society failed this test and gave in to the serpent's tongue. They were spellbound and beguiled by the serpent.

Robert Roos, a member of the European Parliament representing the Netherlands, also stated, "Pfizer's admission actually dismisses the entire legal basis for any and all covid passports that led to massive institutional discrimination as people lost access to essential parts of society. I find this to be shocking, even criminal. This is scandalous. Millions of people worldwide felt forced to get vaccinated because of the myth that 'you do it for others.' Now, this turned out to be a cheap lie. This should be exposed."

The vaccine was not created for covid, but covid was created for the vaccine. Many of us discerned this from the start and had to suffer the ridicule and ignorant bashing from those who trust in government, corrupt leaders, and their insolent mouthpieces, instead of common sense. We should have known the fix was in when all dissenting voices were unilaterally censored and ousted on social media. What is even more astounding is how so much of the truth has been revealed about this great deception and federal, state, and local leaders are still pushing this fake vaccine. This is most definitely the greatest crime against humanity, but the more truth comes out about it, the more docile the public becomes.

This vaccine was so safe that the government wants everyone to take it except illegal immigrants, postal workers, Congress, the White House staff, federal judges, and employees of the Center for Disease Control (CDC), and the World Health Organization

(WHO). Did you know that the COVID-19 vaccine has caused more deaths, hospitalizations, and adverse side effects than all other vaccines combined? Follow that science.

THE BATTLE FOR HUMANITY

Dr. Carrie Madej received her medical degree from Kansas City University of Medical Biosciences in 2001. She currently dedicates her time educating others on vaccines, nanotechnology, and human rights via multiple platforms and speaking engagements. This excerpt comes from the video titled "The Battle for Humanity" by Dr. Carrie Madej, *Why Vaccines Alter DNA*:

"Why are so many successful treatments for Covid-19 being banned from so many countries? Why have thousands of doctors' and healthcare professionals' information concerning Covid-19 been removed from social media platforms without warning?

The Covid-19 vaccine uses a modified RNA or DNA. Why is this important? Because it can potentially alter our DNA our genome. And what's the big deal about DNA or RNA. The genome is what makes us human and separates us from the rest of the plants and animals in the world. It's the blueprint for what creates us, how we reproduce, how we function, how we repair, how we evolve. So, one little change, one little protein taken out can actually create a genital defect or a hereditary disorder. So, something that can alter, that can really be devastating on us, humans. They are proposing using this technology and part of this is called "Transfection" – GMO Technology. Transfection is the same technology used to make a genetically modified organism such as a tomato or corn and they are not as healthy as the organic or wild type that you see out in nature. So, if this is the same technology being use on plants, what will happen to us humans? Potentially, we would not be as healthy. I want to remind everyone that this is the first time that this would be used on humans on a large scale. We would be the experiment. We would be the lab rats. We do not have long term studies.

One of the front runners for this vaccine was *Moderna*. *Moderna* was given one million dollars by the government for this research and development. *Moderna* is backed by the *Melinda and Bill Gates Foundation*. *Moderna* are "the new kids on the block" and have not been around that long. They have never developed a human vaccine nor human medicine ever. This is their first run at it. They fast tracked this experiment. They went from a lab experiment to phase two on forty-five human subjects in sixty-three days (two months). That's crazy. We should have years behind that. When they introduced this high dose vaccine to the forty-five human subjects, one hundred percent had systemic side-effects. Eighty percent of the group that received the low dose had systemic side effects. One of the ways they would apply the vaccine would be to use a bandage called *Micro Needle Platform*. You would get this in the mail, and you would apply this on your hand and then remove the sticker, and you would have a vaccine by doing it yourself. The bandage has tiny little micro needles on it and it's designed after a snake or viper feign and it's like a bite from a snake but many of them. They say you will not feel it but it goes into your system. It would either be the DNA or RNA vaccine. Within the vaccine would be something called *LUCIFERACE*. This is very important to know. They've patented an enzyme called *LUCIFERACE*. They claim it's called this because it gives a bio-luminous light. If you have a special application on your smart phone and scan over the place where it

THE SERPENT & THE CROSS

was applied, it will light up. It will show a pattern, a digital code, a bar-code. We're going to be branded. Each person will have their own I.D. This will be in there because they want to hold proof that you have been vaccinated and you will be able to be scan and show proof that you've gotten the vaccine.

Next, there is a Hydrogel. It is a technology that was invented by DARPA (Department of Advance Research Project Agency). This is a small part of the Pentagon's department of defense. This is a special technology that goes under the skin. The body doesn't reject it and it has nano-technology which are microscopic robotic organisms. So, these microscopic organisms that is robotic will be in your body. They can assemble, disassemble and reassemble and do innumerable things to the body. The idea for this is to gather information from your body like your blood pressure, your blood sugar, your heart rate, which sounds good. However, is also has potential to be used for other things like how many steps you've taken, if you've fallen, if you're swimming, if you're running, if you're menstruating, how your menstrual cycle goes, if you're having sex, if you're sleeping. It has the potential to know your own emotions. All of this

120

data, twenty-four hours a day, seven days a week, three-hundred and sixty-five days a year is being accumulated. And where is it going? They claim it's going to a smart app, your phone, the I-cloud or any smart device. But who is getting this information? Who is using it and what are they using it for? These questions have not been answered.

The other important thing to know is they are gathering all of this information about us, and we are being connected to artificial intelligence not just a vaccine. Just like your smart phone, you can send a text, you can send an email, and someone can send something back to your phone. This means they can send something back to our bodies; messages, information. What could happen from that? You can be affected in your mood or behavior or memory. That could really cause a lot of problems and confusion. And who's in charge of this? The Department of Defense? Bill and Melinda Gates? We don't have answers yet. This is something real to know. This is being proposed. This is the loss of autonomy, the loss of independence and the loss of privacy. This is the beginning of something that is called the *Unique Identifier*, this branding, this tattoo. This means the end of cash, the end of credit cards, this is beginning of all of this.

The company is also claiming that Hydrogel has the ability to be a drug on demand delivery system. This means that through a light application, a drug can be delivered into your body. This is concerning because I know if I take a tablet. I have a bottle that has a label and I take the tablet and I know I'm in control. They literally can activate something in your body. What if you don't know it has been activated? Can you imagine the implications of this? What if people are rioting out of control? Can something be released to sedate you? Is this part of the reason why the military is involved? We need to be critical thinkers and know what they are putting in these vaccines. It is not just a vaccine they're giving us. They are manipulating our DNA, our genome. They say it is temporary, but when you manipulate the genome with transfection, you can make it permanent, and they won't know it until they have done it to everyone vaccinated. Do you want to take that chance?

The Covid-19 vaccines were being pushed by the number one vaccine dealer in the world, Bill Gates. He has absolutely no medical education. He is the number financer of the W.H.O. and he dictates their policies. In March of 2017, Bill Gates sat down with President Donald Trump in the White House where President Trump was interested in establishing a commission to look into the ill effects of vaccines because Robert Kennedy Jr. had advised him to do so. Bill Gates told Trump not to do that. Bill Gates said that getting into the vaccine business was the best business decision he ever made. His wealth went from 50 billion to 100 billion."[12]

VII

DIAMONDBACK DEMOCRATS

Carol Swain, Professor of Political Science and Law at Vanderbilt University wrote *The Inconvenient Truth About the Democratic Party*:

"When you think about racial equality and civil rights, which political party comes to mind? The Republicans? Or the Democrats? Most people would probably say the Democrats. But this answer is incorrect.

Since its founding in 1829, the Democratic Party has fought against every major civil rights initiative and has a long history of discrimination. In 1857, in the Supreme Court case, Dred Scott v. Sanford, the court ruled that slaves aren't citizens; they're property. The seven justices who voted in favor of slavery? All Democrats. The two justices who dissented? Both Republicans. The Commander-in-Chief during the war to free the slaves was the first Republican President, Abraham Lincoln (who changed from Democrat to Republican). Lincoln's vice president, a Democrat named Andrew Johnson, assumed the presidency. But Johnson adamantly opposed Lincoln's plan to integrate the newly freed slaves into the South's economic and social order. Johnson and the Democratic Party were unified in their opposition to the 13th Amendment, which abolished slavery, the 14th Amendment, which gave Blacks citizenship, and the 15th Amendment, which gave Blacks the vote. All three passed only because of universal Republican support.

During the Era of Reconstruction, federal troops stationed in the South helped secure rights for the newly freed slaves. Hundreds of Black men were elected to southern state legislatures as Republicans, and twenty-two Black Republicans served in the U.S. Congress by 1900. The Democrats did not elect a Black man to Congress until 1935.

But after Reconstruction ended, when the federal troops went home, Democrats roared back into power in the South. They quickly reestablished White Supremacy across the region with measures like Black Codes – laws that restricted the ability of Blacks to own property and run businesses. And they imposed poll taxes and literacy tests, used to subvert the Black citizen's right to vote. And how was all of this enforced? By terror – much of it instigated by the Ku Klux Klan, founded by a Democrat, Nathan Bedford Forrest. As historian Eric Foner, himself a Democrat, notes, 'In effect, the Klan was a military force serving the interests of the Democratic Party.'

President Woodrow Wilson, a Democrat, shared many views with the Klan. He re-segregated many federal agencies, and even screened the first movie ever played at the White House – the racist film *The Birth of a Nation*, originally entitled *The Clansman*. A few decades later, the only serious congressional opposition to the landmark Civil Rights Act of 1964 came from Democrats. Eighty percent of Republicans in Congress supported the bill. Sixty one percent of Democrats did. Democratic senators filibustered the bill for 75 days, until Republicans mustered the few extra votes needed to break the logjam. And when all of their efforts to enslave Blacks, keep them enslaved, and keep them from voting had failed, the Democrats came up with a new strategy: if Black people are going to vote, they might as well vote for Democrats. As President Lyndon Johnson was purported to have said about the Civil Rights Act, 'I'll have them niggas voting Democrat for two hundred years.'

So now, the Democratic Party prospers on the votes of the very people it has spent much of its history oppressing. Democrats falsely claim that the Republican Party is 'the villain', when in reality it's the failed policies of the Democratic Party that have kept Blacks down. Massive government welfare has decimated the Black family. Opposition to school choice has kept them trapped in failing schools. Politically correct policing has left Black neighborhoods defenseless against violent crime. So, when you think about racial equality and civil rights, which political party should come to mind?"[1]

THE SERPENT & THE CROSS

On December 3, 1867, President Andrew Johnson said this in his annual message to Congress, "Negroes have shown less capacity for government than any other race of people. No independent government of any form has ever been successful in their hands. On the contrary, wherever they have shown a constant tendency to relapse into barbarism.

The suppression of the Black vote was always fought vigorously and even fought with violence and death by the Democratic Party. On September 28, 1868, White men in Opelousas, a city in St. Landry Parish, Louisiana, killed around two hundred and fifty people, mostly Black Americans. The goal was to suppress turnout among Black voters (and anyone who supported Reconstruction efforts).[2]

The serpent's spellcasting, forked tongue has even been able to get an entire country of Black people to support and vote for the very political party and wicked system who enslaved, murdered, and perpetually committed inhumane atrocities against Black people, time and time again. And what's worse, is that if you attempt to have a fact-based conversation about this with many Black people, they immediately become emotional, upset, and defensive. This is how effective the lie becomes over time, when even the truth actually strengthens the lie!

If by some miracle the Democratic Party had a change of heart and reversed their policies toward Black people, that would be one thing. However, the truth is that the Democratic Party of murder and treachery has not changed at all. Just like serpents, they do not change their nature, just their skins. Every season, snakes shed their old skins and come forth with new skins. In other words, they are able to "reinvent themselves." After the Civil Rights Movement, many Democrats realized they could not defeat the Republicans, so they joined them. This is why today White Supremacy extreme groups are called "right wing" and the Democratic Party daily accuses Republicans of being White Supremacists, Neo Nazis, and racists. This was the work of the serpent's forked tongue and without question, the Democratic Party (who committed hundreds of years of terrorism against Blacks), was magically able to successfully divert all American racial sins to the Republicans. And through the power vehicle of "bought and paid for" corporate media, this lie is repeated so often on a daily basis that the ignorant actually believe it. The mainstream media uses White Supremacy so often now, that it has little to no real affect and most Americans have become numb to it. Their false prophets of baal (media personalities) even call Black people, who disagree with their extreme views, "White Supremacists."

Stockholm Syndrome

The Stockholm Syndrome is a coping mechanism, that people in abusive situations and captives use.[3] These people develop positive feelings toward their abusers or captors over time, and a psychological condition occurs when the victim of abuse identifies and attaches, or bonds, positively with their abusers. This syndrome was originally observed when hostages (who were kidnapped), not only bonded with their kidnappers, but also fell in love with them. Black Americans suffer from this Stockholm Syndrome because the majority of them have not only developed positive feelings toward the very people and political party who abused them for hundreds of years, but they have fallen in love with them to the point where they actually become irate and sometimes violent in defense of their allegiance to them. There is an unfounded loyalty to this demonic political party and if you ask the typical Black person why they vote Democrat, they cannot give you a rational answer. I usually ask my fellow Black Americans, "What political party enslaved us, and fought against our rights every step of the way?" Instead of answering this very simple question, they usually pause for a moment and then spew something ridiculous like, "Oh my goodness, please tell me you're not a Trump supporter!"

This blind loyalty to the party who has destroyed Black Americans goes so deep that when you look at many of the failing inner cities of America, one hundred percent of the time, they are run by Democrats. The mayor, city council members, district attorney, police chief, board of education members, and many others who hold offices all belong to the Democratic Party. However, somehow whenever election season comes around, these Democrats campaign openly about how it is the Republicans who are to blame for every one of their failed policies, high crime rate, high unemployment, lack of jobs, dilapidated and failing schools, and billion dollar deficit. Chicago is a prime example. There is not one Republican on the city council or in any position of authority within the city. However, Republicans are always the political pinata whenever election season comes around. It is mind boggling.

As we look at the condition of inner cities in 2022, while Democrats control the Presidency, House, Senate, and run many major cities, the Stockholm Syndrome is glaringly more obvious. Because of far left, Democratic district attorneys, who have defunded the police departments (which are needed the most in Black neighborhoods), opened the borders, and grossly lacked policies on bail and law enforcement, crimes like murder, rape, and theft have skyrocketed. No group of people have suffered more under these lawless policies than the Black community. However, somehow when the season comes around to vote and remove these Democrats from office (the very people and system who continue to terrorize them), Black people in substantial numbers still re-elect the very snakes who are the perpetual perpetrators of the Black community's demise. These are the results of the serpent's evil forked tongue. satan is "the prince of the power of the air." He controls the airwaves and mass media outlets. As long as the people continue to tune into his lying tongue and remain inoculated with deception, stupidity, and fear, they will never see the real enemy for who he is. Turn off CNN, MSNBC, ABC, CBS, and open your Bible. If the serpent has your ear, he has your mind.

REPARATIONS

Reparations are systems of redress for egregious injustices. Native Americans received land and billions of dollars from the federal government for various benefits and programs because they were forcibly removed from their native lands. America paid $1.5 billion to Japanese Americans who were interned during World War II.[4] The United States via the Marshall Plan, helped to ensure that Jews received reparations for the Holocaust. West Germany agreed to pay $3.45 billion Deutsch Marks in 1952 to Holocaust survivors.[5] On November 23, 2022, Joe Biden agreed to pay one billion in climate reparations to poor, undeveloped nations for damage caused by America's use of fossil fuels.[6] African Americans are the only group that have not received reparations for state sanctioned racial discrimination.

America attempted to atone for slavery right after the Civil War. Union leaders concluded that each Black family should receive 40 acres. General William T. Sherman signed Field Order 15 and allocated 400,000 acres of confiscated confederate land to Black families.[7] Additionally, some families were to receive mules left over from the war. This is where we get "40 acres and a mule." The Republican Party was founded to combat slavery and racism, as clearly seen in their national party platforms of 1856 and 1860. In 1860, Abraham Lincoln won the Republican nomination and became president. President Abraham Lincoln signed the Emancipation Proclamation on January 1, 1863, which declared that all slaves in confederate-held territory would be "thenceforward and forever free."[8] Unfortunately, on April 14, 1865, President Lincoln was assassinated and Vice President Andrew Johnson, who was a Democrat, became the next president. President Johnson reversed Field Order 15 resulting in the land being returned back to former slave owners. Former slave owners were paid reparations for lost property and Blacks had to return to sharecropping to till the same fields for the former slave owners. Imagine that - giving reparations to the racists for loss of property and not the people who were enslaved.[9] America is thirty trillion dollars in debt and print money out of thin air but still has not paid reparations for the greatest evil the country ever committed. Slavery was a democrat institution. Jim Crow racist laws was by the democratic party. The Democratic party should pay the reparations to African Americans.

STUPIDITY BY BONHOEFFER

In the darkest chapter of German history, during a time when incited mobs threw stones through the windows of innocent shop owners, and women and children were cruelly humiliated in the open, Deitrick Bonhoeffer, a young pastor began to speak publicly against the atrocities that the regime had produced. After years of trying to change peoples' minds, Bonhoeffer came home one evening and his own father had to tell him that two men were waiting in his room to take him away. In prison, Bonhoeffer began to reflect on his country of poets and thinkers and wondered how they had turned into a collective of cowards, crooks, and criminals. Eventually, he concluded that the root to the problem was not malice, but stupidity. In his famous letters from prison, Bonhoeffer argued that stupidity is "the more dangerous of the good than malice," because "while one may protest against evil, it can be exposed and prevented by the use of force. Bonhoeffer said, "Against stupidity, we are defenseless. Neither protest nor the use of force can accomplish anything here. Reason falls on deaf ears. Facts that contradict the 'stupid person's' prejudgment are simply not believed, and when they are irrefutable, they are just pushed aside as inconsequential and incidental. In all this, the 'stupid person' is self-satisfied and being easily irritated, he becomes dangerous by going on the attack. For that reason, greater caution is called for when dealing with 'a stupid person' than with a malicious one. If we want to know how to get the better of stupidity, we must seek to understand its nature. This much is certain, stupidity is in essence not an intellectual defect but a moral one. There are human beings who are remarkably agile intellectually but 'stupid' and others who are intellectually dull yet anything but 'stupid.' The impression one gains is not so much that stupidity is a congenital defect but that under certain circumstances people are 'made stupid' or rather they allow this to happen to themselves. People who live in solitude manifest this defect less frequently than individuals in groups. And so, it would seem that stupidity is more a sociological problem than a psychological one.

It becomes apparent that every upsurge of power, be it of a political or religious nature, infects a large part of humankind with stupidity, almost as if this is a sociological, psychological law where the power of the one needs the stupidity of the other. The process at work here is not that particular human capacities such as intellect suddenly fail. Instead, it seems that the overwhelming impact of a rising power, results in humans choosing to be deprived of their inner independence and more or less consciously, they give up an autonomous position. The fact that 'the stupid person' is often stubborn must not blind us from the fact that he is not independent. In conversation with him, one virtually feels that one is dealing with him, not at all as a person, but with slogans, catch words, and the like that have taken possession of him. HE IS UNDER A SPELL, blinded, misused, and is abused in his very being, having thus become a mindless tool, 'the stupid person' will become capable of any evil, and incapable of seeing that it is evil. Only an act of liberation, not instruction can overcome stupidity.

Here, we must come to terms with the fact, that in most cases, a genuine internal liberation becomes possible only when external liberation has proceeded it. We must abandon all attempts to convince 'the stupid person' until then."[10] Bonhoeffer died due to his involvement in the plot against Adolph Hitler, at dawn on the 9th of April 1945, at Flossenberg Concentration Camp just two weeks before soldiers from the United States liberated the Camp. "Actions spring not from thought, but from a readiness for responsibility," Bonhoeffer once said, "The ultimate test of a moral society is the kind of world that it leaves to its children."

The Democratic Party is not only anti-Christ but anti everything freedom. Because we have allowed them to control most of the powerful institutions in America, they no longer even desire to campaign and pontificate their ideas in order to commandeer our vote. They yearn to possess power, indefinitely, and monopolize the political arena. The progressive left of the Democratic Party has seized control of the party and they are anti-free speech, using shadow banning, censorship, and blacklists. If Elon Musk had not bought Twitter and exposed the company's wide, extreme bias and corruption, most Democrats would not believe that all the censorship was happening. Unfortunately, this season of deception has produced a majority who does not even care about the corruption, because they have been convinced that extreme action is necessary and justified in order to keep their political opponents out of power. If conservative ideas are so toxic and dangerous, Democrats should want everyone to hear them, so that they can make a sound decision when it is time to vote. However, the very opposite is true with Democratic leaders. They do not want the public to hear common sense, rational, law-abiding, pro-family, pro-religious, pro-American ideas, and policies. They just want the public to believe whatever the Democratic Party tells them is the truth, because that is exactly how tyrannical powers behave. They would rather silence mainstream, positive viewpoints than debate them. They prefer to suppress the truth about themselves, while they amplify the lies about their opponents.

DOUBLE STANDARD DEMON-CRATS

Today's Democratic Party hate their own constituents. They hate America, all of her liberties, and everything the Word of God upholds. They believe we are ignorant, and do not possess the proper faculties to govern ourselves. We have to accept the blame for some of these beliefs. Look at how we fall for their constant bombardment of "race-baiting" and "identity politics." This is the power of the serpent's tongue. Many have lost all common sense, and like the Pied Piper, they are enchanted by the sound of music, and without any resistance, simply follow it to their own demise. They are the main ones who scream, "race," for any and all circumstances, while it is the Democratic Party who are the true racists and have been from the beginning of this Republic. They are the definition of gaslighting. They are the epitome of projection. Everything they accuse their opponents of, they are themselves to their very core. The Democrat elites in power never expect to live by the laws and policies they promote for us. Illegals do not live in their neighborhoods. Crime is not out of control within their gated communities. They push to limit our access to firearms while they can afford

THE SERPENT & THE CROSS

private security. They closed our schools while their children went to private schools. They mandated that we lockdown and wear masks and all the while they continued to dine at restaurants without masking. They are double standard demon-crats. It is no laughing matter how America has gotten to this point, how obvious the tricks of the serpent are, and how lost millions are to his tactics. The True Church of Yeshua is the only answer and vanguard to the serpent's tongue because we possess God's tongue of Truth, the Word of God.

PROGRESSIVES & CONSERVATIVES

It is one thing to send your sons and daughters off to be indoctrinated and brainwashed by America's liberal, Christ-hating, and America-hating colleges and universities. However, it is another thing when you are willing to pay the absolutely astronomical price tags attached to it. Actually, paying for the insane indoctrination of our children from all that is righteous, biblical, and wholesome is nothing less than insane, and it is astounding how many so-called, "Christian homes" are doing exactly this. I have heard several liberal professors explain the meaning of progressivism and conservatism from a historical perspective and it was nothing less than lies. They insinuated how progressives desire to progress ideas, family, government, and culture within the society, while conservative ideology desires to conserve past ideas and standards for family, government, and culture. On the surface, this is not too far from the truth. However, it is the spin they later attach to it, that are outright lies. They accuse conservatives of desiring to conserve America's past racist, hateful, segregated, and oppressive ways, while progressives are champions of progressing past America's horrific history into a more inclusive, equal, and equitable future. This is where the serpent's forked tongue takes root. Remember that both liberals and progressives are part of the Democratic Party.

The wicked Democratic Party who is responsible for the slavery, racism, hate, segregation, murder, and oppression of Black people in America, somehow miraculously became Born Again, and washed clean of their sins while their evil history was appointed to the Republican Party. This is what they convince their gullible students to believe: that the Democratic Party, who is 100% guilty of the worst of America, was supernaturally absolved of their heinous past and deeds, and they now desire to progress above and beyond them, while simultaneously, somehow, making the Republicans guilty of things they never did to Black people and blaming them of yearning to "conserve" slavery, racism, hate, segregation, and oppression of Black people.

The truth is, progressives are manipulators of words, as we witness daily among the "woke" elites of today. Progress is not really progress, but in reality it is what most decent, law abiding, common sense people would call "regression" and "oppression." "Progress" to progressives are rights and absolute protections for:

- the LGBTQ+ community
- murder of innocent life in the womb, and even past birth
- drag queens preaching the gospel
- drag queens teaching our children in school (labeling parents as domestic terrorists for disagreeing with state-funded perversion in schools)
- allowing adolescents to choose what sex to identify as

- state-funded gender reassignment surgeries for children
- the sexual indoctrination of our children in public schools
- high taxes to pay for climate change initiatives
- total dependency on government and the destruction of free markets and capitalism.

The list above is just the "tip of the iceberg." "Progressive" sounds nice. However, for the Democratic Party, it actually advocates everything the Bible forbids and the very diabolical practices that brought Divine judgement on nations throughout the Scripture. And "Conservativism" is not for conserving and protecting the dehumanizing practices of the Democratic Party (which makes no sense for a Republican to conserve practices they did not participate in), but rather the desire to conserve the rights in the U.S. Constitution, America's Judeo–Christian foundation concerning religion, the core family structure, small government, low taxes, reduced government spending, free markets, and deregulation. However, the truth is not what your sons and daughters are going to learn in America's liberal institutions.

CLIMATE CHANGE COBRA

This quote comes from Paul R. Ehrlich, the population biologist. It was printed in *The New York Times* in 1969:

"The trouble with almost all environmental problems, say that by the time we have enough evidence to convince people, you're dead . . . We must realize that unless we are extremely lucky, everybody will disappear in a cloud of blue steam in twenty years."

In 1970, *The Boston Globe* published an article titled, *Scientist Predicts a New Ice Age By the Twenty-First Century:*

"Our pollution may obliterate the sun and cause a new ice age in the first part of the next century . . . if the current rate increase in electric power generation continues, the demands for cooling water will boil and dry the entire flow of the rivers and streams in the continental Unites States . . . By the next century the consumption of oxygen in combustion processes, worldwide, will surpass all of the processes which return oxygen to the atmosphere."

In 2006, former Vice President Al Gore said:

"Unless drastic measures to reduce greenhouse gases are taken within the next 10 years, the world will reach a point of no return."

In 2019, Representative Alexandria Ocasio-Cortez said:

"The world is going to end in twelve years if we don't address climate change. This is our World War II."

Should and can we do better taking care of the planet? Of course. But if nothing changes as of right now, the Earth will be just fine, and nothing catastrophic will happen to mankind because of it. Mankind's greatest problem is sin, and the rejection of Christ, not climate change. Witchcraft is the worship of the Earth through magic, sorcery, and casting spells. This is the core of baal worship, and the Democratic Party is its priesthood. What was once known as global warming but rebranded as climate change, after being debunked, is the Democrats' religious hierarchy. There is no climate crisis. The only real crisis is stupidity as we quietly allow our corrupt government to use our hard-earned tax dollars to fund the Democratic Party's witchcraft called "climate change." Fear is one of the serpent's greatest weapons of mass destruction, and mass distraction. He used fear to get the world to obey him during this "plan-demic" season. He is using fearmongering to get free people to willingly advocate senseless, fake science to coffer hundreds of billions of dollars to line the pockets of a few elitists who continue to sell us lies in order to keep them richer. Just like the Jehovah Witnesses, who falsely predicted (on several occasions), the coming of the Lord (after selling all their possessions), and waited for Him to crack the sky, these global warming, I mean climate change false prophets are doing the same and using the weapon of global death and destruction to get you to comply. They are currently willing to destroy the economy of first world nations and their energy independence by getting rid of nuclear energy and the use of fossil fuels. All over the world is this made up, existential threat called "climate change." How many times will we allow them to predict a date of global catastrophe and when it does not happen, allow them to continue the ruse? We cannot be this stupid!

MASS MAIL-IN BALLOTING

During the "plan-demic," the Democrats initiated their trump card called mass mail-in balloting. This form of voting that is ripe with the potential of corruption and coercion was their fail-safe plan to beat the big, bad "orange man." Although Nancy Pelosi, Chuck Schumer, and other major Democratic leaders, once openly spoke ill concerning the dangers of mass mail-in balloting, their opinion suddenly changed once the "plan-demic" began. The media also promoted mass mail-in balloting and scared many voters from going out in public to vote. During the 2022 midterms, something that has never been witnessed in politics occurred. Democratic leaders refused to debate their Republican opponents. The Democratic Secretary of State in Arizona, Katie Hobbs, who was twice convicted for discrimination against two African American women, and also participated in "Black-face" during her high school's mocked version a slave auction, was behind in the polls by eleven points the day before the Arizona Gubernatorial 2022 Election. However, somehow Katie Hobbs won the race. How? When you know the fix is in, you do not have to debate your opponent. Liberal local and national

THE SERPENT & THE CROSS

media and liberal social media platforms suppressed the story of Hobb's blatant racism, just like they suppressed the Hunter Biden story when it came out during the 2020 Presidential Election. When asked by media why Hobbs would not debate her opponent, Kari Lake, Hobbs stated that Kari was "mean and a bully with terrible ideas" and she did not want to "share a stage" with her. The media responded to Hobbs by stating that it was her responsibility to show her constituents how to stand up to bullies. However, Hobbs replied that she would not. Hobbs did not take the risk of being exposed by her opponent during a public debate because she knew her supporters did not know the truth about her racism. In addition, her supporters would find out the truth about her demonic Democratic ideas and would face a true acid test by being displayed next to conservative ones and Hobbs could not risk that. She understood that the system was already rigged in her state, so she simply sat it out and let the corrupt mass mail-in balloting take its course. Until laws are passed to change the legality of mass mail-in balloting, the Democratic Party will continue to harvest ballots in the twenty-five states where it is legal.[11] They have devised a way to stay in power no matter how many people physically turn out to vote.

FUNDAMENTALLY TRANSFORM AMERICA

On October 30, 2008, on the cusp of his historic presidential election, then Senator Barak Obama stated, "We are five days away from fundamentally transforming the United States of America."[12] Millions of Americans cheered as history was made with the first Black American elected to the highest office of the land. Barack Obama is African and American but not an African American because he is not a descendant of American slavery. His father was African and his mother American. Likewise, Kamala Harris is not African American. She's a woman of color (father is Jamaican and mother is Indian) but did not come from slaves; on the contrary, her family owned one of the largest slave plantations in Jamaica. But of course, the cancel culture conveniently overlooked this fact. My point is, America will never allow a descendant of American slavery to sit as president. People of color may celebrate the election of black people into high office in America, but there is a method to their madness. The Caucasian powers that be absolutely care about whether or not a black candidate for president is from slavery or not. They will not have someone they believe to be a "nigga" (descendant of slaves) lord over them. This is why Jesse Jackson, who was the best candidate, was not the Democratic nominee when he was a candidate for the Democratic presidential nomination in 1984 and then again in 1988. He is an African American!

When Barack Obama spoke of fundamentally changing America, it did not come with any sort of definition or outline. We had to wait and see. Well, guess what? We can see clearly now what all it entailed and there is nothing wholesome or righteous about it. Hope and change were the framework, but totalitarianism is the ideology that fundamentally transforms. The textbook definition of totalitarianism is "to seek to fundamentally transform human nature via some form of political ideological cultural upheaval." This of course, comes within the parameters of marriage, family, and sexual orientation. We have witnessed this take place since he took office until the present, like never before. This transformation is seen in the perversion within society and the culture. Obama got it started and his then vice president, Joe Biden

THE SERPENT & THE CROSS

is finishing the job. Let's look at this great transformation.

CHILD SACRIFICE

The fundamental transformation of America is actually baal worship and the number one component of this wicked practice is child sacrifice. Old Testament baal worship required its followers to offer their newborn babies to the false god baal. This meant you placed your baby boy/girl on the scorching hot altar of the image of baal and witnessed your newborn scream in unfathomable agony until its death. Although abortion was around years before Barack Obama and Joe Biden's presidency it has expanded its practice to lengths not previously seen. Did you know that there isn't one Democratic congressperson or senator who is not for late term abortion? These baby murders first argued that life in the womb wasn't a human until birthed and that it was just fetal tissue. Today their godless ideology has pushed the envelope to revealing their true nature as they're attempting to pass laws where women can murder their child up to thirty days after birth. This was never about women's healthcare or "Planned Parenthood." It was always about baal worship and sacrificing the most innocent and precious part of humanity (the unborn) to demon spirits. Any follower of Christ who supports this treacherous murderous practice wouldn't know Christ if He appeared right before them.

SEXUAL PERVERSION

The party of diversity and inclusion has another definition for diversity and inclusion which has eluded most people who believes in freedom and righteousness. These woke ideologues want to control speech and one way to accomplish this is by changing the language and flooding our vocabulary, and in essence reality, to secure their domination. Here are a few woke words which will explain what I mean. War means peace. Freedom is actually slavery. Him or her is "they." Ignorance is strength. Inclusion is exclusion. A mother is a "birthing person", and boys can be "girls" and vice versa.

Democrats say they are for women but somehow this equates to no longer believing in the two genders of male and female. How do you properly celebrate the first female vice president when your party cannot define what a woman is? Democrats state they're for women and women rights while simultaneously allowing men who simply claim they're transgender to join women's sports where they are absolutely dominating the women. Thirty-nine-year-old New Zealander, Laurel Hubbard, a transgender weightlifter, broke two female weightlifting records at the world championships in 2017. Laurel lived as a man for thirty-five years then broke female weightlifting records at thirty-nine years old.[13] Someone who is biologically, one hundred percent male can simply identify as the opposite sex (which they cannot define) and be permitted to participate and dominate women sports. How is this advocating for women? Transgender MMA fighter, Fallon Fox, broke her female opponent's skull in an MMA fight.[14] Gender identity is not subject to how we choose to identify. It is unequivocal defined in our biology. If you dig up the grave of a person one hundred years after their death you will be able to easily identify what sex, they were. God made this fact undeniable regardless of what we choose to identify as. A man will always biologically, be a male no matter how much of his anatomy he mutilates. God created male and female, marriage, and the Church. It doesn't matter how fallen man attempts to alter, pervert, or change them. We did not create them, and we will never have the power to change them. All attempts will end in Divine judgement and retribution as it did during Noah's flood and the judgement of Sodom and Gomorrah and the cities of the plain.

Demetrius Minor who is now Demi Minor, a transgender woman who was incarcerated in a New Jersey prison, got two female inmates pregnant.[15] The ACLU is aggressively fighting legal battles for trans people to have the right to serve their time in whichever prison they desire. This baal worship has penetrated our penal system and now we have women who identify as men incarcerated in men's prison and men who identify as women incarcerated in women's prisons. This is INSANITY! This stupidity produces a new set of problems as women are coming up pregnant in the women's prison by transgender women and transgender men are being sexually assaulted in men's prisons. What's more astonishing than all of this nonsense, is how afraid many in the Church are and will not even speak out about it.

The same Democrat hypocrites who yelled, "Believe all women," during the Supreme Court confirmation of Judge Brett Kavanaugh, became mutes shortly after presidential candidate, Joe Biden was accused of sexual assault by Tara Reade. The same Democrats who demand a woman has total autonomy of her body and the right to murder her child in the womb changed on a dime once the Covid-19 vaccines were released to the public as they demanded that all Americans get the vaccine and villainized anyone who refused to take it. In other words, we have autonomy of our person unless they tell us differently. This is the party of satanic insanity. The Democratic Party is the political party who has perverted the public school system with witches and members of the LGBTQ community in order to indoctrinate the next generation with their sick ideology. Democrats support the public-school administrations' new rules that allow children to self-identify as any gender of their insane gender spectrum and permit them to go into any bathroom they choose. They are the ones placing feminine napkins in boys' bathrooms. The serpent purposes to pervert everything God created, especially His highest creation of mankind. This is all baal worship and the Democratic Party is the serpent's priesthood. This is no longer about Democrats and Republicans. None of us are born in a political party. But it is evident that it is about good and evil today, light and darkness, righteousness, and wickedness. There is no gray area, no straddling the fence here. Get right or get left.

Emma Colton of Fox News reported December 11, 2022

"A retired navy seal who became famous nearly ten years ago after coming out as transgender announced that he is detransitioning and called on Americans to 'wake up' about how transgender health services are hurting children.

"Everything you see on CNN with my face, do not even believe a word of it," Chris Beck formerly known as Kristin Beck, told conservative influencer Robbi Starbuck in an interview published earlier this month. "Everything that happened to me for the last ten years destroyed my life. I destroyed my life. I'm not a victim. I did this to myself, but I had help."

"I take full responsibility," he continued. "I went on CNN and everything else, and that's why I'm here right now. I'm trying to correct that."

Beck gained notoriety in 2013 when he spoke with CNN's Anderson Cooper about transitioning to a woman.

"I was used . . . I was very naïve, I was in a really bad way, and I got taken advantage of. I got propagandized. I got used badly by a lot of people who had knowledge way beyond me. They knew what they were doing. I didn't," he said during an interview.

Beck said he's speaking out about transgenderism to protect children in the current political climate, where there are gender clinics "over all of America."

"There are thousands of gender clinics being put up over all of America," he said. As soon as (kids) go in and say, 'I'm a tomboy or this makes me feel uncomfortable' and then a psychologist says, 'oh, you're transgender.' And then the next day you're on hormones – the same hormones they are using for medical castration for pedophiles. Now they are giving this to healthy 13-year-olds."

"Does this seem right?" he asked. "This is why I'm trying to tell America to wake up."

Beck said that when he began transitioning, it took just an hour-long meeting at Veterans Affairs to be offered hormones.

"I walked into a psychologist office and in one day I have a letter in my hand saying I was transgender. I was authorized for hormones. I was authorized all this other stuff," Beck said.

"I had so much going wrong in my system when I started taking those," he added. "Some of that was paid by the VA, and I'm sorry to the American people that I did that."

Beck said he has been off hormones for about seven years now.

"This is a billion-dollar industry between psychologists, between surgeries, between hormones, between chemicals, between treatments," he continued. "There are thousands of gender clinics popping up all over our country. And each of those gender clinics is going to be pulling in probably over $50 million."[16]

THE SERPENT & THE CROSS

TRANSGENDER TRAGEDY

On February 1, 2023, *Joe Rogan Experience* podcast with guest Jordan Peterson discussed gender surgeries in the United Kingdom. This clip is entitled *All Hell's Gonna Break Loose.* Jordan Peterson states:

"It was just released with the *Tavistock* staff; you know *Tavistock* closed down in the UK. It was the big gender surgery performing institute in the UK. The government closed it down because they figured out in the UK that, Wow! The rates of transgender transformation requests were skyrocketing, and even the people at the clinic knew that they were rushing people along the transformation pipeline way faster than they should've without proper clinical evaluation. There's a thousand lawsuits out against them (*Tavistock* in the UK now), out of thirty thousand transition processes.

America is still where the UK was four years ago. We have not woken up to the fact that all hell's going to break loose on this front with people like Chloe Cole launching lawsuits. That's the only thing that's ever going to stop this: lawsuits or jail sentences. It's absolutely appalling. This is also part of the reason I felt I've been at war for like six months. Ken Zucker in Toronto, he is the world's leading authority on transgenderism. He divided it into two parts. The autogynephilic types, the guys who get sexual kicks from dressing up in women's clothing and go do drag queen story hour, say well, "We're just pristine and pure.' No, you're not. You're getting a sexual kick from dressing up in women's clothing. And let's not Bloody well forget it.

And you can't even say that now but every clinician worth his salt knew that for decades. And then there's another sub population and those are gender non-conforming kids and like a conservative skeptic might say, 'There's no such thing.' No there is. So, your typical gender non-conforming kid would be feminine boy or masculine girl who's high in trade openness, and who's also high in neuroticism. And there's lots of kids like that. And so they don't fit in that well with their peer group. And some of them develop body dysphoria. They are not very happy with themselves at puberty because they don't fit in. But Zucker showed very clearly, he ran a transgender clinic at Cam H in Toronto for decades, and he was one of the world's leading authorities in terms of publications I think he was the editor of the *Lead Journal* for years. They just took him out in Canada: fired him, and disgraced him, and he battled on the lawsuit front for like ten years, and was eventually vindicated, but he didn't have a political bone in his body. He was a clinician through and through. He wasn't playing political games. Documenting autogynephilic, just clinical reality. Now it's become revolting to even suggest such a thing. 'Oh, there's nothing sexual about this.' Yeah, right! You're dressing up in lingerie before your mirror at home, tucking your penis between your legs, imagining you have a vagina, for a sexual kick. Oh, there's nothing sexual about that. Yeah, right! Bloody, absolute liars.

Then you have the kids that don't fit in on the gender front. That's a different pathway. But with them, if you leave them alone (so do no harm) ninety percent of them accept their body, their sex, age eighteen or nineteen. And eighty percent of them are gay. So what that also means is most of the kids being sterilized and mutilated are gay. Eighty percent of them. So, I don't see how the LGBT alliance is going to hold up under that sort of reality.

Let's add something equally ugly to it since we haven't gone far enough yet. So here, we'll do a little bit of arithmetic. Awhile back, a *Disney* executive mentioned on video, this is when Florida went after *Disney*. I think she was head of *Domestic Programming* for *Disney*. She said, 'I have two children, five and seven. One is "trans," and the other is "pansexual".' And I just thought mathematically, the chance you have a "trans kid" is one in three thousand. That's not a very high chance. Let's say the chance that you have a "pansexual kid" is the same, whatever *pansexual* means. I don't even know how to calculate those odds. But whatever that is, is rarer than trans because no one ever even heard about it until five years ago. So the joint probability that you have a "trans kid" and a "pansexual kid" is one in nine million. The odds that you're a pathological, narcissist sacrificing your own children to the glorification of your compassion is eight million, nine hundred and ninety-nine thousand, nine hundred and ninety-nine to one. So do you have a "trans kid" and "pansexual kid" or are you a "devouring mother?" Well, you can look at the odds and decide for yourself.

Freud was no dummy when he pointed to the fact that the "devouring mother" was one of the major impediments to proper human development. He knew that. Looking deep into the darkest families and seeing this proclivity of the overprotective mother to destroy the developing integrity of the child, to keep the child infantile, to cling to that relationship, instead of developing life for herself and letting the child go flourish. That's Hansel and Gretel, right? You're lost in the woods; why? Well, your family is broken up. You have an evil stepmother and now you're lost in the woods. What's your abuse rate if you have a stepparent? One hundred times normal. You're lost in the woods. What happens? You come across a gingerbread house. Well, that's pretty convenient. You need a house. It's more than you can even hope for. It's not just a house. It's a house made out of candy. Well, what's inside a house made out of candy? A witch who wants to fatten you up and eat you. And that's the "devouring mother" and that's an old fairytale.

One of the things we won't honestly discuss in our society is the fundamental nature of female political psychopathology. There's male political psychopathology, obviously. That's what the feminist complains about all the time when they talk about the oppressive patriarchy and toxic masculinity. There's no shortage of toxic masculinity. So, is there any toxic femininity? Well, not if the feminist is just the oppressive, virgin goddess. Yes, there's female, political pathology. The tendency to infantilize everyone, and the tendency to assume that everyone who doesn't go along with infantilization is properly characterized as a predator. You wonder why the universities are turning into extended daycares? A lot of the reason for that is: women who don't have anything better to do than turning the university students into infants they never had."

PARTY FOR PEDOPHILIA

The next letter for the LGBTQ+ community is P for pedophilia. Since Elon Musk's takeover of *Twitter*, he has banned more than 44,000 accounts that belonged to people who promoted child pornography. This means that before Musk's acquisition of the social media platform, *Twitter* enabled this wickedness, openly, while simultaneously, intentionally, shadow-banning, and censoring thousands of Conservatives. This shadow-banning, and censoring occurred predominantly during the 2020 election among conservatives who did absolutely nothing wrong. They simply held conservative views. Yoel Roth, *Twitter's* Head of Trust and Safety (who was fired by Musk), in his doctoral dissertation entitled *Gay Data*, argued that minors should have access to *Grinder*, an adult male "gay" hook-up app. Yoel was a part of the overlords of "free speech" at *Twitter*, while never lifting a finger to remove pedophilia, and child porn on the site. However, he did move "Heaven and Earth" to fact-check every independent and conservative post.

What is known as the *Twitter Files* has exposed the coordinated effort of *Twitter* executives and the FBI to collude in silencing any voice on *Twitter's* platform that did not line up with their sick ideology. Ninety-eight percent of *Twitter's* employees donated to the Democratic Party. This means the entire platform was systemically biased, and *Twitter* hired people based upon these guidelines. It cost Musk forty-four billion dollars to purchase *Twitter*, and thus far it is worth every single penny, as the Democrats' far left agenda is being exposed every day. You can't find any Democrats in D.C. openly speaking against any of the sick perversions their party advocates today. Everything sick, twisted and perverted that we've witnessed enter our culture came from the Democratic party.

Mississippi, Alabama, and Arizona are the only three states that do not allow gender procedures on children. Forty-seven states promote gender affirming care for minors. Why would a country ever need drag queens to read to children? America has fallen. Once we allow the serpent's sick and twisted sexual perversions into our culture, there is no way to purge it out. Just like yeast in flour, you cannot sift it out. The only remedy after this wickedness is deeply rooted in a society is to allow that nation to fall and be destroyed like Sodom and Gomorrah. There has never been a country who allowed these heinous sexual perversions in their culture and were able to successfully remove them. You can stick a fork in America because she is done. It is just a matter of time now. The good news is that she is ripe for harvest and if only the Church understood who they are in Christ and were about the Father's business, we would see the handwriting on the wall, and preach the Gospel of the Kingdom of Heaven like never before. The harvest is plenteous, but the laborers are few.

BALENCIAGA & BAAL

The fashion brand Balenciaga has openly promoted pedophilia in their ad campaigns. The media reported it, then moved on. However, when the media deals with anyone who disagrees with the corrupt, evil agenda of the serpent's forked tongue, they are willing to go back thirty years to dig into a person's past to find something, so that they can cancel them. Where is the outcry to cancel a fashion brand who publicly celebrates the sickest of all perversions, pedophilia?

On Balenciaga's homepage, there are two caution tapes on a table with Balenciaga's name on it. However, there is a variation in its spelling. They added an extra "a" in their name, spelling, "BAAL-ENCI-AGA." This is their homepage and nothing on it is by accident. They did not accidentally misspell their name and why is it on caution tape? The answer is because the devil is not hiding anymore, and we still do not see him. The serpent understands how America's culture is so compromised that he can hide in plain sight. They intentionally added "baal" in their name because that is the ancient demonic god they worship. Baal worship required child sacrifices and it is the Democratic Party who promotes and defends the murder of innocent life in the womb.

The teacher's unions in America fund the Democratic Party with millions of dollars so that they can promote sodomy, perversion, and the serpent's sexual revolution to our children, starting from the time they attend public school. Out of one-hundred English teachers in America's public schools, ninety-seven are Democrat. Out of one-hundred Health teachers in public schools, ninety-nine are Democrat. Math and Science teachers are eighty-seven Democrats out of one-hundred. Every evil policy the Democratic Party advocates institutes baal worship in the country. One of Balenciaga's main designers has an Instagram page full of satanic imagery and child sacrifices. Balenciaga is owned by the French multinational corporation, Keiring, and Keiring owns Bottega Veneta, Gucci, Alexander McQueen, and Yves Saint Laurent.

Biden's Blasphemous Bosses

Joe Biden prides himself in making history as the most diverse president but when evil and perversion come under the umbrella of diversity, you can keep it. The party of slavery, racism, KKK, Jim Crow, and murder has attempted a satanic facelift with their push for equity and diversity, but it is all a smokescreen to push baal worship in our culture. Democratic politics is based on "judging a book by its cover," instead of the other way around. They are experts at identity politics, race baiting, and divisiveness. Promotion for them is not based on merit or qualifications, as we know it. On the contrary, skin color is their only qualification today, and it is used to deceive the public, while all the while the stooges they choose are absolutely incompetent, but they qualify for the Democratic Party based on their race, "political correctness," and "diversity list."

1. Kamala Harris is the first female vice president and woman of color. She checked the Democrats' race and sex box and is a kackling, incompetent, embarrassing, disappointment.

2. Katanji Brown Jackson is the first African American, female, supreme court justice. She said that she could not define what a woman is and has a judicial record of giving the lightest sentences possible to convicted pedophiles.

3. Karine Jean-Pierre is the first black, homosexual, immigrant, female press secretary. She is the most incompetent and "confused at the podium" press secretary in history.

4. Peter Buttigieg is the first homosexual transportation secretary who was on maternity leave, without anyone knowing it, while America was in the midst of a supply chain crisis. He has thus far, refused to even visit the victims of the

catastrophic, chemical spill caused by the Norfolk & Southern train derailment in Palestine, Ohio. Another absolutely incompetent, Democrat shell.

5. "Rachel" Leland Levine is the first transgender assistant secretary for health. He is a four-star admiral in the *Unites States Public Health Service Commissioned Corps.* He would not give an answer during his Senate Confirmation Hearing when asked By Senator Rand Paul about genital mutilation ("gender affirming care") procedures. Senator Paul asked Levine if he believed that a minor was capable of making life-changing decisions, such as changing one's sex. Of course, the man dressed in a wig and dress would not answer because he believes that a child has the "right" to mutilate his/her genitals without parental consent.

I could go on and on with the list of incompetent, perverted, Christ-hating political hacks that Joe Biden has appointed to his cabinet. If each of these people served America with honor and integrity, I would be fine with it. However, one can tell by their actions, that not one of them has good intentions for American citizens. They know they were not chosen to serve us. They serve the devil's sadistic, sinister agenda of perversion and death. The leaders of today's Democratic party are the loudest to recite America's racist and murderous history while always conveniently leaving out how they were the actual perpetrators of said atrocities. Instead of putting forth policies that genuinely help African Americans, they simply promote Black, symbolic, figure heads into office, who will do zero to advance the Black agenda in America. Nonetheless, they continue to receive up to ninety-two percent of the Black vote and at this point, black people cannot blame anyone but themselves for this insanity. Joe Biden said it best when he stated "if you have a problem figuring out whether you're for me or Trump, then you're not black."

Blacks Bailed-out Biden

Joe Biden was pretty much out of the race for the Democratic nomination until James Clyburn gave him his endorsement three days before South Carolina's state primary. Clyburn, the House majority whip and the highest ranking African American in Congress, is one of the major reasons why this blundering, buffoon is in office. Roughly sixty percent of all Democratic voters in South Carolina are Black. Exit polls indicated that nearly half

Democratic primary voters in South Carolina said Clyburn's endorsement was an important factor in their vote and twenty-four percent said it was the most important factor. After Biden's landslide win in South Carolina, Joe hugged Rep. James Clyburn and said "You brought me back." Therefore, it was a Black politician who resuscitated the presidential run of a known bigot who lied about marching in the Civil Rights movement and getting arrested while trying to meet Nelson Mandela. Biden is the racist who wrote the Clinton Crime Bill that single-handedly began Black Mass Incarceration. He's the liar who was publicly embarrassed out of the 1988 presidential run for plagiarism. Biden, who is the real white supremist, did the eulogy for Robert C. Byrd, a known racist and KKK member. Biden is the same racist who said "Unlike the African American community, with notable exceptions, the Latino community is an incredibly diverse community with incredibly diverse attitudes about different things." The world believes the African American community is a monolith politically because that is exactly what we've shown them over and over by our vote. The Black vote is more powerful than we truly understand. It's time to wake up!

THE FOREST AND THE AXE

The Forest was shrinking but the Trees kept voting for the Axe, for the Axe was clever and convinced the Trees that because his handle was made of wood, he was one of them. *Turkish Proverb*

This proverb is a perfect example of the relationship between many African Americans and the Democratic Party. Why we keep voting for the axe that cuts us down, I'll never know. This is so obvious to see that one would need help not to understand it. It is time to get off the "Democrat Plantation." It would be better for African Americans not to vote at all, then to participate in the political system by voting for the people who arrogantly show their disdain for us, and then spit in our faces immediately after apprehending our vote by doing absolutely nothing that benefits our communities. The first job of any government is to protect its citizens. Look at the crime rate in most Democrat ran cities and it tells you everything you need to know. Albert Einstein said "Never confuse education with intelligence." If you don't know what that means just look at the leaders of the Democratic party.

VICTIMIZATION VENOM

The racial divide and tension in America's society is attributed to Democrats' power over media and their obsession with race, tribalism, and class warfare. Victimhood has become a curse in Black America. The far-left Democrat-ran media, uses race, racism, and white supremacy, so often that we cannot recognize it when it genuinely happens today because everything is racist. Millennials have been thoroughly indoctrinated with victimhood and anti-American sentiment because Democrats control education, media, social media, and the entertainment industries. Democrats are the only ones yelling, "Systemic Racism," while never admitting it was and is their political party and ideology who invented every system of racism in American culture.

There is racism, no matter what country you live in. We cannot legislate morality, but we can control how we respond to racism, and it is not by labeling everything that happens to us, "racist." This victimhood mentality only produces weak, co-dependent, and complaining, people. When you see yourself as a victim, you will never confront the real problems in your life and become a victor.

If you are a part of the leadership in the Democratic Party, you are not allowed to openly disagree with them. Their blind loyalty does not come from a place of honor and integrity, but like any kingdom of darkness, unity is a commandment, or you will be dismissed and publicly humiliated. It does not matter how despicable the words or behavior of a Democratic leader, are, their fellow Democrats and Democrat-ran media will never break ranks or speak independently. It is only when such a person has been deemed by the leadership of the party as "useless" that in perfect unison, the party and media throw them overboard. The Democratic National Committee (DNC) is a dictatorship. If you go against the king, you will be executed. If you do not completely adhere to their diabolical agenda, you will not receive any funding or assistance from their powerful political machinery to help you campaign and keep you in office. You literally sell your soul to the devil to be a member of this wicked organization. If you are a God-fearing person, who loves justice, and righteousness, you have to agree that everything perverted, unnatural, lawless, and anti-Christ, is exclusively being pushed by the demonic Democratic Party.

Cold War

America is in the midst of a Civil Cold War and history has repeated itself because of the racist, violent, murderous, extreme, Democratic Party who have caused it, just as they caused the Civil War. Conservative college students are never the ones who form mobs to scream, curse, and become violent toward visiting speakers who have differing opinions and worldviews. It is not conservatives who daily push to censor the free speech of their opponents. We did not witness major cities burned down at the hands of free thinking or conservative groups during the aftermath of George Floyd's death. We did not witness independent or conservative politicians publicly asking Americans to donate finances to help release anarchists who were arrested for rioting and violence. However, Joe Biden, Kamala Harris, and other Democrat leaders did. Anytime you tune into a mean-spirited, hate-filled rant from the media, it is usually from the Democratic side of the conversation. This is because whenever one cannot stand on facts, he/she will resort to emotionalism and attack the other party. It was the Democratic President Barack Obama who spied on incoming President Donald J. Trump. It was Democratic President Joe Biden who weaponized America's intelligence agencies against his political opponents. What is most unfortunate about all of this, is that most people who have already been influenced and indoctrinated by the forked tongue of the Democratic Party and mainstream media, have become docile to any and all attacks against other Americans whose beliefs are contrary to them. He who controls the media, controls the minds of the people. Adolph Hitler understood this and was able to manipulate millions of Germans to side with his homicidal agenda and we are witnessing the beginning effects of it in America, right now. The moral and political divide is so thick in America that you can cut it with a knife. The serpent has successfully used his false prophets of baal in media, in getting most Americans so focused on race, color, equity, abortion, red and blue, right and left, and guns, that we fail to realize that none of these issues are the root of the problem. While we are busy pointing the finger at one another, the corrupt elite remain in power, pulling all the strings, and playing puppet master.

These are all fruit of the problem. The root of the problem is the slow tolerance for injustice and evil that we have developed in this last generation and the result is that people lack common sense. In other words, we have become "stupid" and that was the serpent's ultimate goal to begin with.

VIII

FIERY SERPENTS

The deadly poison of the serpent is his bite of sin. One of the ways he seduces us into this trap, is by rousing us to speak against the authority of God and His delegated authority. This rebellion is always at the heart of the serpent's forked tongue and was present in those who built the Tower of Babel. Man's Fall in the Garden of Eden was because the serpent inoculated God's first couple with rebellion. This deadly poison was injected into the children of Israel as they became arrogant enough to speak against God's authority. Numbers 21:5-6 records:

And the people spake against God, and against Moses, Wherefore have ye brought us up out of Egypt to die in the wilderness? for there is no bread, neither is there any water; and our soul loatheth this light bread.

And the LORD sent fiery serpents among the people, and they bit the people; and much people of Israel died.

Out of all the ways God could have scolded His people for their sin, in this special situation, God decided to allow the same serpents that bit them mentally and emotionally to bite them physically. *Fiery* is the Hebrew word *sarap* meaning *burning, poisonous (serpent), symbolic creature from their copper color.*[1] *Serpent* is the same Hebrew word used for the serpent who deceived Eve in the beginning. This is the same burning venom, poison of rebellion, and unbelief that raged through the children of Israel and caused them to openly use their mouth to bite and speak against the Lord and His leader Moses. This story reminds us about how disrespectful and dangerous it is to walk in unbelief, to the point where we begin to speak against God and his leaders. When we doubt God, it is evil because we are questioning His integrity and love for us as Daddy, especially in the case of Israel. Look at the resume God had with them: the great deliverance from slavery in Egypt, the parting of the Red Sea, the giving of the commandments, and the manna that fell from Heaven six days out of the week. They even spoke ill of God's manna by stating, "...*our soul loatheth this light bread.*" Unbelief is a condition of the heart. It would not have mattered how many miracles God performed for the Israelites or how many times he delivered them, they had evil hearts of unbelief and doubted God's love, mercy, and power each step of the way. This is why that generation was rejected from inheriting the Promised Land and died in the wilderness.

We really do not comprehend how poisonous it is to house fear and doubt in our hearts and mouths. Jesus said, "... for out of the abundance of the heart the mouth speaketh." Evil words come from evil hearts. When our mouth burns with the venom from the serpent's tongue, it is because it came from the heart (that is desperately wicked, who can know it?), and this is called "heartburn." Hebrews 3:12 says:

Take heed, brethren, lest there be in any of you an evil heart of unbelief, in departing from the living God.

Psalms 78:40 states:

How oft did they provoke him in the wilderness, and grieve him in the desert!

Hebrews 11:6 exhorts us:

But without faith it is impossible to please him: for he that cometh to God must believe that he is, and that he is a rewarder of them that diligently seek him.

Like many of us, Israel had become used to speaking evil against the Lord and His leader. When we get too casual with our mouth, uttering venom against God's character, we don't realize how close to death we are. This reminds me of the old saying, "With friends like this, I don't need any enemies." Sometimes, we listen to the fear and doubt of the serpent's tongue and do not realize we have been set up for failure. How can we be Believers if we do not believe? Why do we claim to be people of faith when we have no faith? The just shall live by faith and God does not have any justifiable excuses to ever doubt Him. His name is Faithful!

HEALING

Death broke out in the camp when the fiery serpents appeared and began biting the rebels. We do not know how long it took for the people to die from the serpent bites, but death was imminent without Divine intervention. This is also true of mankind since the fall of Adam. We are all born in sin, but we do not have to die in it. We are all born disconnected from the Father, but we do not have to stay in this hopeless predicament. We are born already bitten by the poison and death of the fiery serpent because we are a part of the fallen bloodline of Adam and in Adam all die. However, by God's grace, we are born in time, and within our lifetime we have a chance to accept the message of salvation. This message is seen "in type" in the story of the fiery serpents that bit the children of Israel. Numbers 21:7-9 continues:

Therefore the people came to Moses, and said, We have sinned, for we have spoken against the LORD, and against thee; pray unto the LORD, that he take away the serpents from us. And Moses prayed for the people.

And the LORD said unto Moses, Make thee a fiery serpent, and set it upon a pole: and it shall come to pass, that every one that is bitten, when he looketh upon it, shall live.

And Moses made a serpent of brass, and put it upon a pole, and it came to pass, that if a serpent had bitten any man, when he beheld the serpent of brass, he lived.

No matter what we've done, our loving and gracious Lord simply requires true repentance. It does not matter what way of escape and deliverance God supplies. Any deliverance He grants us begins with humility and repentance. The modern-day Church is slowly moving away from encouraging sinners to verbally repent. We have people group all their sins into one big bunch called, "I repent of my sins." However, we need to be specific and call them out. Even if we cannot remember them all, we surely should try and verbalize our sins because we definitely committed them. There is something restorative about stating aloud before God what we have done to offend His Holiness. Repentance should never be rushed. We should be quick to repent, but never be hasty through the process. The thief crucified on Jesus' right side, who was moments from death, simply repented and acknowledged Who Jesus was. The Scripture says, *"...To day if ye will hear his voice, harden not your hearts."*

God designed healing to be performed in a very scientific way. He instructed Moses to use the very thing that caused the sickness to bring about the healing. It was fiery serpents that bit Israel and brought sickness and death. Therefore, God specifically demanded that a fiery (brass) serpent be used to bring about the deliverance. This is exactly what medical science uses today regarding vaccines. They use the poison from the virus to create a vaccine that will contain the proper antibodies to destroy the virus. What is even more powerful is how God's instructions to Moses was a prophecy of what Jesus would accomplish on the Cross. He Who knew no sin became sin that we might become the righteousness of God in Him. How?

FIERY SERPENT

God instructed Moses to make a fiery serpent and set it upon a pole. Anyone who was bitten had to look upon in order to be healed. The serpent represents sin, and the fire represents the judgement of sin. Moses' presentation of the fiery serpent was a brass serpent and brass represent the judgment of sin in Scripture. Moses had a brazen serpent made and placed it upon his wooden pole. As the rebels in the camp, who were bitten by the fiery serpents, looked upon the brazen serpent on the wooden pole, they were healed from the curse of death. On the wooden cross, Jesus became sin for us. He did not have sin because He was the sinless Lamb of God, but Jesus, as our sacrifice willfully became sin for us. When did He become sin for us? He became sin when He screamed, *"My God, My God, why hast Thou forsaken me?"* He didn't just become sin (the serpent), but He was the fiery (brass) serpent. The fire of God's Divine judgement for the sin of the world struck Jesus and He confessed to this when He yelled, *"I thirst!"* In the story of the rich man and Lazarus, the rich man died and lifted up his eyes in hell, being tormented in a flame. He begged Abraham to have Lazarus dip his finger in water and let a drop of water cool his tongue. Jesus was not only thirsty from hanging on an old wooden cross for hours, but He was thirsty because He had become sin for us and was experiencing the fires of God's judgement upon Him. Ultimately, He was thirsty for the Presence of His Father, because He had never been without His loving Presence. For the first time in His eternal Self-Existence, He could not discern His Father's love. The core of every atom that made all of creation (spiritually and physically) shook as the Creator wailed, *"I thirst!"* His Words sent a ripple through time and eternity. I believe every angel in Heaven fell on their faces at the Words of the Only

Begotten Son of God. We can't even wrap our minds around the reality of His Words. On top of this, to know He was willing to experience separation from His Eternal Father for you and me is beyond all human understanding. This is why we call Him: King, Lord, God, Everlasting One, Wonderful Counselor, Almighty God, Alpha & Omega, the Beginning and the End, and the One True God.

SERPENT EATING SERPENTS

There is a mystery to salvation, and it is hidden within the wealth of Scripture and in the fabric of every story in the Bible. Romans 16:25 says:

Now to him that is of power to stablish you according to my gospel, and the preaching of Jesus Christ, according to the revelation of the mystery, which was kept secret since the world began.

Ephesians 3:4 reads:

Whereby, when we read, ye may understand my knowledge in the mystery of Christ.

1 Corinthians 2:7 states:

But we speak the wisdom of God in a mystery, even the hidden wisdom, which God ordained before the world unto our glory.

Ephesians 1:9 declares:

Having made known unto us the mystery of his will, according to his good pleasure which he hath purposed in himself.

The New Testament is the Old Testament revealed and the Old Testament is the New Testament concealed. God prophesied what would happen at the Cross thousands of years before it happened within the stories of the Old Testament. The possibility and probability of this is beyond human calculation. Another hidden revelation concerning the serpent and the Cross is seen when Moses first presented himself before Pharaoh as God's deliverer of the Jewish slaves. Exodus 7:10-12 records:

And Moses and Aaron went in unto Pharaoh, and they did so as the LORD had commanded: and Aaron cast down his rod before Pharaoh, and before his servants, and it became a serpent.

Then Pharaoh also called the wise men and the sorcerers: now the magicians of Egypt, they also did in like manner with their enchantments.

For they cast down every man his rod, and they became serpents: but Aaron's rod swallowed up their rods.

The serpent and the Cross are the central theme of the Bible. This theme reoccurs in type throughout Scripture and this episode of Moses and Aaron before Pharaoh is one of the most profound ones. The rod that Aaron casts down represents the wooden Cross that the Lord died upon. The rod that became a serpent reiterates the truth of Jesus becoming sin for us. The interesting part of this story is how Pharaoh called for his wisemen, sorcerers, and magicians and how they performed their enchantments. This connects back to the serpent introduced in Scripture in the Garden of Eden and the Hebrew meaning of *serpent: to hiss, to practice divination, to whisper (a magic spell); to prognosticate, and enchanter.*[2] Jesus said, "...be ye therefore wise as serpents, and harmless as doves." Pharaoh called for his wisemen. Today's Church knows how to raise money, throw concerts, have altar calls, and hold Easter egg hunts, but lacks wisdom. Today's Church lacks wisdom to win, wisdom to plan and strategize, wisdom to train and mobilize, and wisdom to take the Gospel of the Kingdom to their jobs, businesses, and secular industries.

The serpent's power is his tongue, because his tongue practices divination, casts magic spells, prognosticates, enchants, and hisses the poison of lies and sin that controls this fallen world. Pharaoh's wisemen were ancient workers of darkness who contained the serpent's nature at their very core. Pharaoh called these magicians to withstand the miraculous power God demonstrated through Moses and Aaron, as their rod became a serpent. This was a direct insult to Pharaoh and also a challenge given by God to the "great Pharaoh," who wore the graven image of a serpent on the front of his crown. When Moses' rod supernaturally turned into a serpent, God was directly challenging, not only Pharaoh's authority as a god himself, but it was also a direct challenge to the serpent god that the Egyptians worshipped. In essence, Moses, Aaron, and God, Himself, were calling out Pharaoh and satan. God came to the enemy's house and challenged their greatest symbol of power.

Pharaoh had the home court advantage, and the upper hand because he had access to his wisemen, magicians, and sorcerers. The very serpent that was proudly connected to the center of Pharaoh's miter, was presented in a grand display, supernaturally, by God, right in Pharaoh's house. God was not playing! This was "in your face, I'm not afraid of you," gamesmanship at its best.

Prophetically, God was exhibiting that He was emphatically ready to deal with sin. When the rod became a serpent, the gloves were taken off and all bets were off. God came to "throw down" and He brought the fight to Pharaoh. This was an Old Testament picture of the events that would occur at the Cross of Calvary. Jesus came on the enemy's turf, born as a man, and was tempted in all points, but found without sin. Jesus brought the fight to the serpent. Sin and death are the serpent's strength. The serpent and sin are synonymous. Just as Moses' rod became a serpent, on the Cross, Jesus became sin for us. In the process of becoming sin for us, part two of the showdown took place. Pharaoh's magician's, sorcerer's, and wisemen's enchantments caused their rods to turn into serpents also, but God's serpent swallowed all of their serpents. The Scripture does not inform us how many of the enemy's serpents there were, but we do know God's rod that became a serpent swallowed every one of them. *Swallow* is the Hebrew word *baw-lah* that means *to make away with, to destroy, devour,* and *eat up.*[3] When Jesus became sin for us, He swallowed all the enemy's serpents (at the same time). He *made away with, destroyed,* and *devoured* all the power of the serpent. 1 John 3:8 says:

. . . For this purpose, the Son of God was manifested, that he might destroy the works of the devil.

Colossians 2:14-15 says:

Blotting out the handwriting of ordinances that was against us, which was contrary to us, and took it out of the way, nailing it to his cross;

And having spoiled principalities and powers, he made a shew of them openly, triumphing over them in it.

The serpent was ignorant to the truth and revelation of the Lord becoming sin, and how it would be the weapon that destroyed the power of sin over fallen man. 1 Corinthians 2:6-8 informs us:

Howbeit we speak wisdom among them that are perfect: yet not the wisdom of this world, nor of the princes of this world, that come to nought:

But we speak the wisdom of God in a mystery, even the hidden wisdom, which God ordained before the world unto our glory.

Which none of the princes of this world knew: for had they known it, they would not have crucified the Lord of glory.

As Moses' rod that became a serpent, swallowed Pharaoh's sorcerers,' magicians,' and wisemen's serpents, it pointed to Jesus becoming the serpent of sin on the Cross for our sins, and in doing so, swallowing, and spoiling the principalities and powers of the serpent and triumphing over them in it. Had the serpent knew the hidden wisdom of God in this, he would not have had Pharaoh's servants cast down their rods into serpents, and he would not have crucified Jesus. What the enemy meant for evil, God's hidden wisdom turned for good. From the very beginning in the Garden of Eden, the serpent reared his ugly head in the affairs of man, and our journey to the Cross (road) was destined. Because God is All-Knowing, the Scripture is clear that God ordained man's salvation from the foundation of the world. God created the enemy as the serpent, and even he did not fully understand why, until Jesus said, *"It is finished,"* and the manifold, hidden wisdom of God was revealed. The serpent is formidable and has seduced the entire world through his hissing, magic, spellcasting, divination-working, and lying forked-tongue, but as wise and cunning as he is, he didn't realize he was just a pawn on God's chessboard. The serpent did not know he was playing checkers while God was playing chess. While the serpent was impressed playing god of this world, God is seated high above the Heavens, having seen the end from the beginning, laughing all the way. Our love and trust should be secure in knowing that there is nothing too hard for our Lord. Paul said it best in 1 Corinthians 15:55-57:

O death, where is thy sting? O grave, where is thy victory?

The sting of death is sin; and the strength of sin is the law.

But thanks be to God, which giveth us the victory through our Lord Jesus Christ.

IX

SNAKE VENOM

Evidence has come to light concerning COVID-19 and snake venom. This worldwide "plan-demic" did not accidently breakout. It was a part of the enemy's master plan. Gain-of-function researchers in Wuhan, China were not incompetent and careless. They meticulously released this deadly virus on the world and informed us that this virus came from a beast ("Beast" is the name of the anti-Christ). Genesis 3:1 says, *"Now the serpent was more subtil than any beast of the field . . ."* It is definitely not a coincidence that COVID-19 is closely related to snake venom. Think about this. The serpent unleashed a deadly virus on the planet that operates just like snake venom in the human body. We cannot make this stuff up!

University of Arizona Researchers Find Link Between Covid Deaths and Snake Venom

By Ashley Paredez, Award-winning Journalist with ABC15 News in Phoenix, AZ.

September 1, 2021

Tucson, AZ "Snakes are starting to play a big role in COVID-19 research. Scientists from the University of Arizona have discovered an enzyme, similar to one found in rattlesnake venom, which could be driving COVID-19 deaths.

'We found evidence that there was an enzyme, a snake-like enzyme, in the blood of people who were in extraordinarily high levels,' says Dr. Floyd Chilton, the senior author of the study with the University of Arizona College of Agriculture and Life Sciences. Scientists have worked on this study for the past year and a half. It was recently published in the Journal of Clinical Investigation. The snake-like enzyme is found in healthy people at low levels to prevent bacterial infections. In severe cases of COVID-19, it is doing the opposite.'

'These high levels of this enzyme are looking at those tissues in the organs and saying, you look like a bacterium, let's shred your membranes. Let's put these organs out of their misery,' says Dr. Chilton.

Dr. Chilton says that what's even more remarkable is where we can go from here in the fight against the pandemic. 'Can we come up with specific therapeutics that will not care which variant is coming toward it? Can we come up with specific therapies to address this devastating disease?' asks Dr. Chilton.

Researchers explain that current clinical trials on snake bites are helping in those efforts. They can possibly repurpose some of the treatments being tested. This could one day result in a viable option, other than vaccines, to prevent death in severe patients.

'That allows us to take a precision medicine approach to the disease. We can go into clinical trials and choose the people who are at risk of this mechanism and then, specifically treat people,' says Dr. Chilton.

Their hope, regarding the next step, is an international multi-center clinical trial. They are working with global organizations to see how they can make that possible.

ABC 15 asked a rattlesnake expert for his take on the study:

'For something that is almost universally loathed, as rattlesnakes, it seems fitting, interesting, and ironic, that the venom that they have in rattlesnakes, might be the key in getting out of this situation,' says Bryan Hughes, owner of Rattlesnake Solutions."[1]

By Rosemary Brandt, Researcher

College of Agriculture and Life Sciences at the University of Arizona. August 24, 2021

"Researchers have identified what may be the key molecular mechanism responsible for COVID-19 mortality – an enzyme related to neurotoxins found in rattlesnake venom.

An enzyme with an elusive role in severe inflammation may be a key mechanism driving COVID-19 severity and could provide a new therapeutic target to reduce COVID-19 mortality, according to a study published in the Journal of Clinical Investigation.

Researchers from the University of Arizona, in collaboration with Stony Brook University and Wake

Forest School of Medicine, analyzed blood samples from two COVID-19 patient cohorts and found that circulation of the enzyme secreted, phospholipase A2 group IIA or sPLA2-IIA, may be the most important factor in predicting which patients with severe COVID-19 will eventually succumb to the virus.

This sPLA2-IIA enzyme, which has similarities to an active enzyme in rattlesnake venom, is found in low concentrations in healthy individuals and has long been known to play a critical role in defense against bacterial infections, destroying microbial cell membranes.

'When the activated enzyme circulates at high levels, it has the capacity to shred the membranes of vital organs,' says Dr. Floyd Chilton, senior author on the paper and director of the University of Arizona Precision Nutrition and Wellness Initiative in the university's College of Agriculture and Life Sciences.

'It's a bell-shaped curve of disease resistance versus host tolerance,' says Chilton, a member of the university's BIO Institute, 'In other words, this enzyme is trying to kill the virus, but at a certain point it is released in such high amounts that things head in a really bad direction, destroying the patient's cell membranes and thereby contributing to multiple organ failure and death.'

'Together with available clinically tested sPLA2-IIA inhibitors, the study supports a new therapeutic target to reduce or even prevent COVID-19 mortality,' says study co-author, Maurizio Del Poeta, a Suny distinguished professor in the Department of Microbiology and Immunology at the Renaissance School of Medicine at Stony Brook University.

'In this study, we were able to identify patterns of metabolites that were present in individuals who succumbed to the disease,' said lead study author, Justin Snider, an assistant research professor at the University of Arizona Department of Nutrition, 'The metabolites that surfaced revealed cell energy dysfunction and high levels of the sPLA2-IIA enzyme. The former was expected but not the latter.'

An Enzyme With a Bite

"The sPLA2-IIA enzyme has been the subject of study for half of a century, and it is 'possibly the most examined member of the phospholipase family,' Chilton explained.

Charles McCall, lead researcher from the Wake Forest School of Medicine said that the study refers to the enzymes as a 'shredder' because of its known prevalence in sever inflammation events, such as bacterial sepsis, as well as hemorrhagic and cardiac shock.

Previous research has shown how the enzyme destroys microbial cell membranes in bacterial infections, as well as its similar genetic ancestry with the key enzyme found in snake venom.

The protein 'shares a high sequence homology to the active enzyme in rattlesnake venom and, like venom coursing through the body, it has the capacity to bind the receptors at neuromuscular junctions and potentially disable the function of these muscles,' says Chilton.

'Roughly, a third of the people develop long term COVID-19, and many of them were active individuals who now cannot walk 100 yards. The question we are investigating now is: If this enzyme is still relatively high and active, could it be responsible for part of the long term COVID-19 outcomes that we are seeing?' Chilton goes on to explain."[2]

This is what Dr. Bryan Ardis said about the Covid shots containing snake venom (venomous peptides):

"Like the Johnson & Johnson shot - They're just injecting you with the spike proteins. Now what were the spike proteins? The spike proteins were actually found to be venomous peptides or rabies virus sequences. These weapons are designed to cross the blood brain barrier and attack, specifically glial cells in the brain stem and nicotinic and acetylcholine receptors."[3]

The serpent had this diabolical plan where he would unleash a deadly virus that came from a "beast," and it would target and destroy the human body from within just like snake venom. The devil is a serpent, and he used the science of the very venom he was created with to steal, kill, and destroy mankind.

X

TREAD ON SNAKES

When Jesus informed His disciples concerning the power He gave them over the enemy, He specifically used the words *"tread on serpents and scorpions, and over all the power of the enemy..."* In another passage, Jesus said that Believers *"shall take up serpents..."* The Lord is reminding us that the devil has always been and forever will remain a serpent. In Genesis chapter three, the serpent lost his legs and in Revelation chapter twelve, the serpent acquired wings and seven heads. The most important detail to acknowledge is that he is still a serpent, whether he is crawling on his belly or flying in the air; he's still a serpent. The interesting fact is that the serpent did not become a red dragon with seven heads until he fell and lost his legs in the Garden of Eden. The serpent had no authority in the higher dimension where the Garden of Eden existed. When the Fall occurred, it affected

THE SERPENT & THE CROSS

everything, and everyone (on Earth). As a result, the serpent became the god of this new fallen world system where sin and death reign.

Luke 19:10 says, *"For the Son of man is come to seek and to save that which was lost."* What was lost? Dominion in the spirit, relationship with God, possessing the image and likeness of God, and being filled with God's Spirit (all of these things) were lost.

As aforementioned, satan is a serpent. He is the first serpent in time, rank, and order. The Scripture does not reference and use the serpent to symbolize him but is absolutely transparent in calling him "the serpent." He is called "satan" and "the devil," but he is the serpent. As we reach the New Testament concerning the serpent and the Cross, the Scriptures become even more emphatic in relation to satan being a serpent. Speaking concerning Believers' authority over satan, Mark 16:18 says, *"They shall take up serpents . . ."* Luke 10:19 states:

Behold, I give unto you power to tread on serpents and scorpions, and over all the power of the enemy: and nothing shall by any means hurt you.

During the Tribulation Period, the book of Revelation prophesies an event between Israel (the woman) and satan (the serpent). Revelation 12:14 says:

And to the woman were given two wings of a great eagle, that she might fly into the wilderness, into her place, where she is nourished for a time, and times, and half a time, from the face of the serpent.

When Yeshua was speaking to a group of Jews who rejected the message that He proceeded from the Father, He replied to them in John 8:41-44:

Ye do the deeds of your father. Then said they to him, We be not born of fornication; we have one Father, even God.

Jesus said unto them, if God were your Father, ye would love me: for I proceeded forth and came from God; neither came I of myself, but he sent me.

Why do ye not understand my speech? even because ye cannot hear my word.

Ye are of your father the devil, and the lusts of your father ye will do. He was a murderer from the beginning, and abode not in the truth, because there is no truth in him. When he speaketh a lie, he speaketh of his own: for he is a liar, and the father of it.

On another occasion, Jesus is speaking to the corrupt religious leaders in Israel and states in Matthew 23:32-33:

Fill ye up then the measure of your fathers.

Ye serpents, ye generation of vipers, how can ye escape the damnation of hell?

The Lord made it clear that Father God has children on Earth and the serpent does also. This was first spoken in the Garden of Eden when God stated that He would put enmity between the woman and the serpent and between her seed and the serpent's seed. This truth is a direct contradiction to everyone who states that all people are children of God. No, they are not. Some will be saved. However, many will not come into the Father's loving arms. Only the Father knows who they are. But it is true that the serpent has children on the Earth. In Jesus' day, He spoke directly to the religious leaders and informed them that their father was the devil and that they were serpents and a generation of vipers. All too often, we will find the seed of the serpent in the Church. The serpent knows he cannot beat the Church, so he joins the Church. He is a master infiltrator and just like he infiltrated the Jews in Jesus' day (particularly the Pharisees, Sadducees, and scribes), the serpent will infiltrate the Church, today. Jesus exposed this truth in His Parable of the Wheat and Tares. The serpent's seed of tares looks like, talks like, and worships like the wheat. However, on the inside his seed is just like him and has his genes. The main difference between wheat and tares is that wheat is edible and nutritious, but tares will make you ill and sometimes cause death.

The Scripture does not refer to satan metaphorically as a serpent. The Bible says that he is a serpent or the serpent. Unlike when Peter used a lion as a simile to satan, he said that satan goes about as a roaring lion, seeking whom he may devour (1 Peter 5:8). The Scripture never called satan a lion, but it says that he goes about *as a roaring lion.* The Bible says over and over that satan is a serpent, not like a serpent or as a serpent, but calls him the serpent. He is the hissing one, and whispering one, who casts magic spells with his forked tongue of deception.

BELT OF TRUTH

One of the pieces of the Armor of God is the belt of truth. Ephesians 6:14 says, to have our "loins girt about with (the belt of) truth." This belt is the one piece of armor that connects the rest of the armor. In other words, if we do not possess and use the truth of God's Word, we will not be able to wear God's armor and use it as prescribed. Truth is at the core of all that we believe and do in Christ. Jesus is the Word and God's Word is Truth. Jesus said, *"I am the Way, the Truth and the Life: no man cometh unto the Father, but by Me."* God's people have always struggled with how to properly deal with the serpent's tongue of lies. The devil's mouth is so powerful that as the god of this world, he has successfully cast a magic spell over most generations since the beginning. However, when The Word was made flesh and dwelt among us, Yeshua revealed how to defeat the serpent's tongue that has spellbound all of humanity. God's Word had a showdown with the serpent's tongue, and Yeshua gave us a Master's class on how to defeat the serpent.

Matthew 4:3-4 records:

And when the tempter came to him, he said, If thou be the Son of God, command that these stones be made bread.

But he answered and said, It is written, Man shall not live by bread alone, but by every word that proceedeth out of the mouth of God.

Whenever Truth battles the lie, all we have to speak is what is written in the Word of Truth, the Bible. There is a sexual revolution in the world right now. How should we confront this demonic attack? We should confront it with the weapon of God's Word, *"It is written."* The public school system desires to indoctrinate our children with perversion and confusion. How should we confront the serpent's tongue? We should confront the serpent's tongue with, *"It is written."* The serpent has gotten many people in our society to believe that they can identify as something other than the gender they were born as. What is the answer? *"It is written,"* is the answer. When we are in the serpent's territory, we should never attempt to philosophize or intellectualize various situations or subjects. All we have to do is attack the serpent's lying forked tongue with the double-edged sword of the Word of Truth and declare, *"It is written."*

In order to successfully wage war and win against the enemy we have to be "dressed to kill" in the Armor of God and it all begins with wearing the belt of Truth. Do not ever leave truth. No matter how many in society side with and agree with the lie, continue to stand on truth. Noah was the only one in his generation who was not deceived by the serpent's forked tongue. In the end, the entire world perished, but Noah's family alone, survived the great flood. What price are you willing and ready to pay, to stand with the Truth? Truth is our foundation and everything else is sinking sand. Truth will always be in the minority, among fallen men, but in the majority in the Kingdom of Heaven, because if God be for us, who can be against us? We just experienced the first wave of the power of the serpent's forked tongue, as we witnessed in real time the entire world fall victim to the "Plan-demic," and this fake vaccine mandate. How many people refused to take the vaccine? They did not take it because they were afraid to or have a healthy mistrust for vaccines, but because they knew it was a lie from the pit of hell and decidedly stood on the Truth of God's Word and said, "No!" How many of us lost friends, loved ones, and careers because we understood that we were under the attack of satan's weapon of mass destruction of lies and stood our ground at all costs? Anyone can walk with Christ when everything is going well, but how many of us are truly "sold out" and willing to die for the Truth? This was a test run and a preview to coming attractions. Many in the Church have failed this test and do not seem to have a problem with the COVID-19 vaccine. I firmly believe that if you were willing to take this vaccine, that we all knew had not been properly tested before being made available to the public, you will be willing to take the *mark of the beast* just to "save your neck." It is "put up or shut up" and all cowards have been revealed. We can no longer conveniently ignore the plethora of Scripture that explains the price we must pay to walk with Christ. Yeshua said that the world hated Him, and the world would also hate us. Stop trying to be friends with the world. The serpent is no longer in the closet, but the Church is. Come out and be accounted for. It is our season to tread on snakes and scorpions and over all the power of the enemy. We were birthed in the Kingdom for such a time as this! All of Heaven is waiting with bated breath to see how we will respond in this generation. Are you a Saint or an "Ain't"? The *Benedict Arnold's* have been exposed in the Kingdom. No one cares what church you attend or don't attend. No one is concerned about your affiliation with a certain denomination. All that matters in this season is, "Are you willing to suffer for Christ?" Are you ready to tread on snakes? Do you know who you are in Christ and who Christ is in you? Do you understand your authority as a citizen of the Kingdom of Heaven? Jesus is our Champion and greatest Hero. On the Cross, He stripped the serpent of his power and made an open show of him. Death where is thy sting? Grave where is thy victory? This is our hour. Grab your sword of the Spirit and get in the fight!

New information is coming out daily about how deadly this experimental gene therapy (aka the COVID-19 "vaccine") is and all of the harmful side effects it causes including pericarditis and myocarditis (heart conditions), cancer, diabetes, infertility, pregnant women having miscarriages, menstrual issues and multitudes of children flooding the emergency rooms across the United States due to almost unbelievable effects of the COVID-19 "vaccine," not to mention the numerous sudden deaths. We always heard about the Sudden Death Infant (SDI) syndrome in babies. However, Big Pharma, health professionals, and government officials do not want to take responsibility for the sudden deaths (due to the vax), that are rampant, now.

Scripture says that good will be called evil and evil will be called good. Those of us who spoke common sense and real science, not science fiction or political science had it right from the beginning. We were called "conspiracy theorists," and "deniers of science" but the truth always gets the last word. If you cut off the head of a snake it will continue to move. This is what happened the morning Jesus was resurrected from the dead with all Power in His Hand after crushing the head of the serpent. Yeshua cut the head off the serpent, yet he still has mobility in this fallen world. But we know the devil is defeated and citizens of the Kingdom of Heaven are triumphant. The righteous are bold as lions. We shouldn't have an escape mentality, begging and hoping for the Lord's return. He left us here to take over and advance His Kingdom. The darker it gets, the brighter we shine. This is our season and our time. Remind this forked tongue devil he's only a serpent and the Lord put him under our feet! Every follower of Christ should wear snakeskin shoes from treading on serpents in this season.

WORD OF THE LORD

2/13/23

Just as it was in the days of Jesus, I am allowing the serpent to do his best, but in the end, on Resurrection Sunday, he found out that what he meant for evil, I turned it for good. Likewise, today, do not be dismayed at all of the serpent's handiwork, but keep your eyes on Me, says the Lord. This is a season of exposure. The sins of America's government and its leaders has reached its threshold and I am exposing them. The deals brokered in darkness is about to come into the light. Wicked men and women in power who sold out their country and its citizens because of greed are about to be revealed. Their deeds are about to be laid naked for all to see because I am cleansing this nation from their evil works. Social media, Hollywood, Media, Politicians, Healthcare, Government agencies, and Universities are all being exposed. The serpent wants you to be distracted by things that does not matter but when I pull the covers from his works there will be no denying it. There is a great shaking on the horizon and it will cause many to know I am Lord. There is a great harvest to be reaped and my remnant will answer the call to action. The fear of the Lord is the beginning of wisdom. It is I who is doing a Great Reset. Watch and see says the Most High.

PRAYER

Heavenly Father, I come to you admitting that I am a sinner. I choose to turn away from sin, and I ask You to cleanse me of all unrighteousness. I believe your Son Jesus, died so that I may be forgiven of my sins and made righteous through faith in Him. I call upon the Name of Jesus Christ to be my Savior and the Lord of my life. Jesus, I choose to follow You and I ask that You fill me with the power of the Holy Spirit. I declare I am a child of God. I am free from sin and full of the righteousness of God. I am saved. In Jesus' Name. **Amen**.

FOOTNOTES

CHAPTER 1 – THAT OLD SERPENT

[1] *Luke 1:46-47* KJV says: And Mary said, My soul doth magnify the Lord, And my spirit hath rejoiced in God my Saviour. www.biblegateway.com/passage/?search=Luke+1%3A46-47+&version=KJV ; Accessed on 7/24/22; In 2008, Bible Gateway became a division of Zondervan, and is, today, a member of HarperCollins Christian Publishing.

[2] *Genesis 3:20* KJV says: And Adam called his wife's name Eve; because she was the mother of all living. www.biblegateway.com/passage/?search=Genesis+3%3A20+&version=KJV ; Accessed on 7/24/22; In 2008, Bible Gateway became a division of Zondervan, and is, today, a member of HarperCollins Christian Publishing.

[3] *Old* is the Greek word *archaios* G744, meaning *original*. G744 is from 746; From *arche*; original or primeval -- (them of) old (time). Blue Letter Bible online: http://www.biblehub.com/greek/744.htm ; Accessed on 7/29/22; ©2022 Blue Letter Bible.

[4] *Archaios* G744 comes from the Greek root word *arche* G746, from G756; (properly abstract) a commencement, or (concretely) chief (in various applications of order, time, place, or rank):—beginning, corner, (at the, the) first (estate), magistrate, power, principality, principle, rule. Blue Letter Bible online: http://www.blueletterbible.org/lexicon/g746/kjv/tr/0-1/ ; Accessed on 7/29/22; ©2022 Blue Letter Bible.

[5] *Arche* G746 comes from another Greek root word *archomai* G756 meaning commence, rule; Middle voice of *archo* (through the implication, of precedence); to commence (in order of time) -- (rehearse from the) begin(-ning). Bible Hub online: http://www.biblehub.com/greek/756.htm ; Accessed on 7/29/22; ©2004 - 2022 by Bible Hub.

[6] *Murderer* means *manslayer*. *Murderer* is a synonym of *manslayer*. "Manslayer." *Merriam-Webster.com Thesaurus*, Merriam-Webster online: https://www.merriam-webster.com/thesaurus/manslayer ; Accessed on 7/24/22; © 2022 Merriam-Webster, Incorporated.

[7] The Hebrew word for heaven (*shamayim*) is a plural noun. https://biblereasons.com/bible-verses-about-heaven/ ; Accessed on 7/29/22; © 2013 – 2022 Bible Reasons.

[8] Carter, Lou; What are spurs on snakes? Last Updated: January 21, 2021; https://www.snakesforpets.com/what-are-spurs-on-snakes/ ; Accessed on 12/25/22; © 2022 SnakesForPets.com.

[9] Researchers: Kvon, Evgeny Z., Kamneva, Olga K., Melo, Uira S., Dickel, Diane E., Pennacchio, Len A., Visel, Axel; Progressive Loss of Function in a Limb Enhancer during Snake Evolution; ARTICLE| VOLUME 167, ISSUE 3, P633-642.E11, OCTOBER 20, 2016; https://www.cell.com/fulltext/S0092-8674%2816%2931310-1 ; Accessed on 12/25/22; Copyright © 2022 Elsevier Inc. except certain content provided by third parties. The content on this site is intended for healthcare professionals.

10 Zug, George R.; Jacobson's Organ; Apr 12, 2018; https://www.britannica.com/science/jacobsons-organ ; Accessed on 12-25-22; Copyright © Britannica.

11 *Jacob* is the Hebrew word *Yaaqob* H3290 and means heel-catcher (i.e. supplanter); Jaakob, the Israelitish patriarch:— Jacob. *Yaaqob* comes from the Hebrew word *aqab* (definition below), H6117 in the Strong's Concordance; https://www.blueletterbible.org/lexicon/h3290/kjv/wlc/0-1/ ; Accessed on 12-25-22. ©2022 Blue Letter Bible.

Aqab is a primitive root; properly, to swell out or up; used only as denominative from H6119, to seize by the heel; figuratively, to circumvent (as if tripping up the heels); also to restrain (as if holding by the heel):—take by the heel, stay, supplant,   and   utterly; https://www.blueletterbible.org/lexicon/h6117/kjv/wlc/0-1/   ; Accessed on 12-25-22; ©2022 Blue Letter Bible.

CHAPTER 2 – THAT ⊙LD SERPENT

1 *Serpent* is the Hebrew word *nakas* H5175 (naw-khawsh'); from H5172; a snake (from its hiss):—serpent. Blue Letter Bible online: https://www.blueletterbible.org/lexicon/h5175/kjv/wlc/0-1/ ; Accessed on 7/29/22; ©2022 Blue Letter Bible.

2 *Nakas* H5175 comes from the root word *nâchash* H5172 (naw-khash'); a primitive root; properly, to hiss, for example whisper a (magic) spell; generally, to prognosticate:- certainly, divine, enchanter, (use), enchantment, learn by experience, indeed, diligently observe. Blue Letter Bible online:

https://www.blueletterbible.org/lexicon/h5172/kjv/wlc/0-1/ ;
Accessed on 7/29/22; ©2022 Blue Letter Bible.

[3] *Prognosticate*, verb transitive [from *prognostic*.] 1. To foreshow; to indicate a future event by present signs. A clear sky at sunset prognosticates a fair day. 2. To foretell by means of present signs; to predict. Webster's Dictionary 1828 online: https://webstersdictionary1828.com/dictionary/prognosticate ; Accessed on 7/29/22; © Copyright 2022 MasonSoft Technology Ltd.

[4] *Subtil* is the Hebrew word *'ârûwm* H6175 (aw-room'); passive participle of H6191; cunning (usually in a bad sense):—crafty, prudent, subtil. Blue Letter Bible online: https://www.blueletterbible.org/lexicon/h6175/kjv/wlc/0-1/ ;
Accessed on 7/29/22; ©2022 Blue Letter Bible.

[5] *'ârûwm* H6175 is the passive participle of *'âram* H6191 (aw-ram'); a primitive root; properly, to be (or make) bare; but used only in the derivative sense (through the idea perhaps of smoothness) to be cunning (usually in a bad sense):- very, beware, take crafty (counsel), be prudent, and deal subtilly. Blue Letter Bible online: https://www.blueletterbible.org/lexicon/h6191/kjv/wlc/0-1/ ;
Accessed on 7/29/22; ©2022 Blue Letter Bible.

[6] Synonyms for the word *mix*.
https://www.powerthesaurus.org/fuse+mix/synonyms ;
Accessed on 12/25/22; Power Thesaurus © 2022.

[7] Yahweh gave us seven (7) holydays to celebrate:
1) Passover
2) The Feast of Unleavened Bread

THE SERPENT & THE CROSS

3) The Feast of Firstfruits
4) The Feast of Weeks (Pentecost)
5) The Feast of Trumpets
6) The Day of Atonement
7) The Feast of Tabernacles.
These holydays or "Feasts of the Lord" can be found in Leviticus 23.
www.biblegateway.com/passage/?search=leviticus+23&version=kjv ; Accessed on 12/26/22; In 2008, Bible Gateway became a division of Zondervan, and is, today, a member of HarperCollins Christian Publishing.

[8] Synonyms for the word *mix*.
https://www.powerthesaurus.org/fuse+mix/synonyms ; Accessed on 12/25/22; Power Thesaurus © 2022.

[9] Yahweh gave us seven (7) holydays to celebrate:
1. Passover
2. The Feast of Unleavened Bread
3. The Feast of Firstfruits
4. The Feast of Weeks (Pentecost)
5. The Feast of Passover
6. The Day of Atonement
7. The Feast of Tabernacles.
These holydays or "Feasts of the Lord" can be found in Leviticus 23.
www.biblegateway.com/passage/?search=leviticus+23&version=kjv ; Accessed on 12/26/22; In 2008, Bible Gateway became a division of Zondervan, and is, today, a member of HarperCollins Christian Publishing.

CHAPTER 3 - SPELLBOUND

[1] The definition of *wilderness* is *eremos* (G2048) and it means *of uncertain affinity; lonesome, for example (by implication) waste (usually as a noun, being implied):-desert, desolate, solitary, and wilderness.* https://www.blueletterbible.org/lexicon/g2048/kjv/wlc/0-1/ ; Accessed on 7/29/22; ©2022 Blue Letter Bible.

[2] *Delivered* is the Greek word *paradidomi* (Strong's G3860) meaning *to surrender,* for example *yield up, intrust, transmit: - betray, bring forth, cast, commit, deliver (up), give (over, up), hazard, put in prison and recommend.* www.godrules.net/library/strongs/gre3860.txt ; Accessed on 12/27/22; ©2022 Blue Letter Bible.

[3] Definition of *spelling* is to *name the letters of in order, also to write or print the letters of in order.* Merriam Webster Dictionary online; https://merriam-webster.com/dictionary/spell ; Accessed on 12/26/22; © 2022 Merriam-Webster, Incorporated.

[4] Kosloski, Philip; What does the word "gospel" mean?; 7/03/20; "[The English word gospel] is very likely derived from the Anglo-Saxon *god* (good) and *spell* (to tell), and is generally treated as the exact equivalent of the Greek *euangelion* (*eu* well, *aggello*, I bear a message), and the Latin *Evangelium,* which has passed into French, German, Italian, and other modern languages. The Greek *euangelion* originally signified the 'reward of good tidings' given to the messenger, and subsequently 'good tidings.'"; https://aleteia.org/2020/07/03/what-does-the-

word-gospel-mean/ ; Accessed on 12/27/22; © Copyright Aleteia SAS.

[5] On April 19, 1882, Charles Darwin died at the age of 73. At the age of 72, Darwin, who "scarcely" left his home, found out that Lady Elizabeth Hope was in the neighborhood preaching the Gospel (she was an evangelist) and he invited her for tea. When Lady Hope arrived, Darwin was reading the book of Hebrews. Here is a short excerpt of their conversation from a published letter, where Charles Darwin begins speaking:
"This is the Epistle of Hebrews; the Royal epistle I call it. Isn't it so? And oh, this Book, this Book, I never tire of it." And he began to comment on some of the great Gospel truths, which I only regret extremely, I cannot give verbatim. He (Darwin) spoke of Christ in this way: "He is the King, the Saviour, the Intercessor, dying, living," and discoursed rather freely, and with great animation on different parts of the subject. "But what about Genesis, the very first book in the Old Testament? Your name is always associated in one's mind with certain doubts about that history – the Creation, I mean your views?"
Here his whole aspect changed. A look partly of anger, and partly of great distress, was on his face, as he closed his hands, throwing them forward, while he said with a sort of groan or sigh: "I was young then. I was ignorant, I was enquiring, searching, trying to find knowledge, I wanted the truth and there... and then." He hesitated, as if he was quite overcome, and burst out with a louder voice, apparently in great displeasure, "They went and made a religion out of it." This published letter is in the book *The Battlefield of Faith* and also reprinted on pages 28-30 of Dr. Paul Marston's paper.

S. J. Bole, *The Battlefield of Faith* (University Park, Iowa: College Press, 1940), 166–68. The letter text is reprinted in the 2002 article "Charles Darwin and Christian Faith" written by Paul Marston. http://www.paulmarston.net/papers/scienceandfaith/darwin_and_christian_faith.pdf : Accessed on 12/30/22.

[6] Napikoski, Linda, *Biography of Norma McCorvey, 'Roe' in Roe v. Wade Case*; August 14, 2019; https://www.thoughtco.com/norma-mccorvey-abortion-3528239 ; Accessed on 7/22/22; ThoughtCo is part of the Dotdash Meredith publishing family.

[7] Singer, Fred S.; Gore's 'Global Warming Mentor' In His Own Words; January 1, 2000; https://www.heartland.org/news-opinion/news/gores-global-warming-mentor-in-his-own-words ;
Accessed online on 7/22/22; Copyright 2023 Heartland Institute.

CHAPTER 4 – BLACK MAMBA BABEL

[1] *Language* is the Hebrew word *sapa* and it is literally translated *lip* in one hundred and twelve places in Scripture. *Sapa* means *the lip* (as a natural boundary); *by implication, language*; etc.; https://www.blueletterbible.org/lexicon/h8193/kjv/wlc/0-1/ ; Accessed on 12/27/22; ©2022 Blue Letter Bible.

[2] *Speech* is the Hebrew word *dabar* meaning *a word; by implication, a matter (as spoken of) or thing, adverbially, a cause:- act, advice, affair, answer, etc.*; https://www.blueletterbible.org/lexicon/h1697/kjv/wlc/0-1/ ; Accessed on 12/27/22; ©2022 Blue Letter Bible.

[3] *Name* is the Hebrew word *sem* meaning, *definite and conspicuous position, an appellation, as a mark or memorial of individuality; by implication honor, authority, character, (in) fame(-ous), named, renown, and report.*
https://www.blueletterbible.org/lexicon/h8034/kjv/wlc/0-1/ ; Accessed on 12/27/22; ©2022 Blue Letter Bible.

[4] *Restrained* is the Hebrew word *basar* meaning *to clip off, to gather grapes, also to be isolated (for example inaccessible by height or fortification):- cut off, (de-) fenced, fortify, (grape) gather(-er), mighty things, restrain, strong, wall (up), and withhold.*
https://www.blueletterbible.org/lexicon/h1219/kjv/wlc/0-1/ ; Accessed on 12/27/22; ©2022 Blue Letter Bible.

[5] *Babel* (Hebrew) *–Babylonia; means gate of Bel; court of Baal, confusion, chaos, vanity; and nothingness;*
https://www.truthunity.net/mbd/babel ; Accessed on 12/27/22; ©2022 Blue Letter Bible.

[6] *Tower* comes from a Hebrew root word *gadal* meaning *to twist, for example to be (causatively make) large, (in various senses, as in body, mind, estate or honor, also in pride):- advance, boast, bring up, exceed, excellent, be(-come, do, give, make, wax), great(-er, come to... estate, things), grow(up), increase, lift up, magnify(ifical), be much set by, nourish (up), pass, promote, proudly (spoken), and tower.*
https://www.blueletterbible.org/lexicon/h1431/kjv/wlc/0-1/ ; Accessed on 12/27/22; ©2022 Blue Letter Bible.

[7] *Confound* is the Hebrew word *balal* meaning *to fodder, to overflow (specifically with oil.); by implication, to mix; to*

fodder:- anoint, confound, fade, mingle, mix (self), give provender, and temper.
https://www.blueletterbible.org/lexicon/h1101/kjv/wlc/0-1/ ;
Accessed on 12/27/22; ©2022 Blue Letter Bible.

CHAPTER 5 – PYTHON PLAN-DEMIC

[1] February 6, 2023, Batya Ungar-Sargon aired a video on *The Hill* titled *How Elites EXPLOITED The Pandemic To STEAL From The Middle Class*: https://www.youtube.com/watch?v=b-Ill0cdDwE

[2] As of November 16, 2022, a total of 12,943,741,540 vaccine doses have been administered; World health statistics 2022: monitoring health for the SDGs, sustainable development goals. Geneva: World Health Organization; 2022. https://www.who.int/publications/i/item/9789240051157 ; Accessed on 12/28/22; License: CC BY-NC-SA 3.0 IGO; © 2022 WHO.

[3] The COVID-19 vaccination will not give you protection against COVID-19 and it will not reduce the spread of COVID-19; https://www.who.int/emergencies/diseases/novel-coronavirus-2019/covid-19-vaccines ; Click on data and go to Reports and click on World Health Statistics; Accessed on 12/30/22; © 2022 WHO.

[4] Dr. Sucharit Bhakdi's quote from *Financial Rebellion* with Catherine Austin Fitts Podcast Interview (on March 26, 2020) is from a book titled *Corona False Alarm? Facts and Figures* by written by Dr. Karina Reiss and Dr. Sucharit Bhakdi; https://live .childrenshealthdefense.org/shows/financial-

rebellion/qeGXsHDoou/audio; Accessed on 8/10/22; © 2016 - 2022 Children's Health Defense.

⁵ Ibid.

⁶ Ibid.

⁷ *The Freedom of Information request on deaths following COVID-19* (FOI 21/918); published on January 20, 2022; https://www.gov.uk/government/publications/freedom-of-information-responses-from-the-mhra-week-commencing-16-august-2021/freedom-of-information-request-on-deaths-following-covid-19-foi-21918; Click on the first link; Accessed on 8/10/22; © Crown copyright.

Also: https://www.gov.uk/government/publications/phe-monitoring-of-the-effectiveness-of-covid-19-vaccination ; Accessed on 12/30/22; © Crown copyright.

⁸ Deaths due to Covid-19 with no pre-existing conditions in England and Wales: For the year 2020, there was a total of 9,400 deaths; https://www.ons.gov.uk/aboutus/transparencyandgovernance/freedomofinformationfoi/deathsfromcovid19withnootherunderlyingcauses ; Accessed on 12/30/22; All content is available under the Open Government License v3.0.

9,400 Covid-19 deaths with no pre-existing conditions https://www.ons.gov.uk/peoplepopulationandcommunity/birthsdeathsandmarriages/deaths/datasets/preexistingconditionsofpeoplewhodiedduetocovid19englandandwales Go to: 2020 (Final) edition of this dataset. Click on the excel spreadsheet. Go to Table 3a and add up the numbers on Line 30. Table 3a All Deaths (Jan-Dec 2020): Home Deaths 928,

Care Home Deaths 3,017, Hospital Deaths 5,351, and Other Location Deaths 136. In 2020, total deaths due to Covid-19 with no pre-existing conditions in England and Wales is **9,432**; Accessed on 12/30/22; All content is available under the Open Government License v3.0.

⁹ Covid-19 deaths with no pre-existing conditions between the ages of 0-64 and age 65 & over https://www.ons.gov.uk/peoplepopulationandcommunity/birthsdeathsandmarriages/deaths/datasets/preexistingconditionsofpeoplewhodieddduetocovid19englandandwales Go to: 2020 (Final) edition of this dataset. Click on the excel spreadsheet. Go to Table 2 and add up Line 7 (England), Column 1 where it says 1,441 deaths and Line 15 (Wales), Column 1 for a total of **1,549 deaths between age 0-64.** Add up Line 7, Column 2 where it says 7,199 and Line 15, Column 2 where it says 642 for a total of **7,841 deaths age 65 and over**; Accessed on 12/30/22; All content is available under the Open Government License v3.0.

Vast majority of Covid-19 deaths involved much older people; *Deaths due to COVID-19, registered in England and Wales: 2020;* https://www.ons.gov.uk/peoplepopulationandcommunity/birthsdeathsandmarriages/deaths/articles/deathsregisteredduetocovid19/2020 ; Accessed on 12/30/22; All content is available under the Open Government License v3.0.

¹⁰ FOIA Data: *The Freedom of Information request on deaths following COVID-19 (FOI 21/918); published on January 20, 2022;* https://www.gov.uk/government/publications/freedom-of-information-responses-from-the-mhra-week-commencing-16-august-2021/freedom-of-information-request-on-deaths-following-covid-19-foi-21918; Accessed on 8/10/22; © Crown copyright.

https://www.ons.gov.uk/peoplepopulationandcommunity/bir thsdeathsandmarriages/deaths/datasets/preexistingconditio nsofpeoplewhodiedduetocovid19englandandwales Go to: 2020 (Final) edition of this dataset. Click on the excel spreadsheet; Accessed on 12/30/22; All content is available under the Open Government License v3.0.

[11] Ibid.

[12] Ibid.

[13] Younes, Jenin; *The Strangely Unscientific Masking of America*; November 27,2020; https://www.aier.org/article/the-strangely-unscientific-masking-of-america/ ; Accessed on 12/27/22; © 2021 American Institute for Economic Research.

[14] The government and powers that be knew that the 65+ age group was the group at greatest risk.
Vast majority of Covid-19 deaths involved much older people; *Deaths due to COVID-19, registered in England and Wales: 2020;* https://www.ons.gov.uk/peoplepopulationandcommunity/bir thsdeathsandmarriages/deaths/articles/deathsregistereddue tocovid19/2020 ; Accessed on 12/30/22; All content is available under the Open Government License v3.0.

[15] By Hogan, Bernadette, Campanile, Carl and Golding, Bruce; *Cuomo nursing home order did cause more deaths, should've been reversed sooner: task force;* June 15, 2021; New York Post; https://nypost.com/2021/06/15/cuomo-nursing-home-order-

caused-more-deaths-task-force/ ; Accessed on 12/30/22; © 2022 NYP Holdings

[16] Goodin, Emily; *US lockdown NOW, crisis till August: Trump says there are '15 days to stop the spread'...*; March 17, 2020; Daily News; https://www.dailymail.co.uk/news/article-8118415/donald-trump-tells-america-lockdown-15-days-stop-coronavirus.html ; Accessed on 12/30/22; Published by Associated Newspapers Ltd.

[17] CDC website; *CDC calls on Americans to wear masks to prevent COVID-19 spread*; July 14, 2020;
The Centers for Disease Control and Prevention (CDC) calmly asked the people to wear masks;
https://www.cdc.gov/media/releases/2020/p0714-americans-to-wear-masks.html ; Accessed on 12/30/22; Source: Centers for Disease Control and Prevention.

[18] Coffey, Laura T.; *School during the pandemic: The Children Who Disappeared*; September 15, 2021;
https://www.today.com/specials/schoolduringpandemic/ ; Accessed on 1/01/23; © 2022 NBC UNIVERSAL.

[19] Chamorro-Premuzic, Tomas and Wittenberg-Cox, Avivah; *How the Pandemic Increased Domestic Abuse And Sexual Violence Against Women*; May 27, 2021;
https://www.forbes.com/sites/tomaspremuzic/2021/03/27/how-the-pandemic-increased-domestic-abuse-and-sexual-violence-against-women/?sh=7928f0d350a7 ; Accessed on 12/31/22; © 2022 Forbes Media LLC.

Torero, Maximo; *The Pandemic Was a Severe Blow for World Hunger. The Recovery Needs to Start Soon*; Aug. 19, 2021;

https://www.barrons.com/articles/the-pandemic-was-a-severe-blow-for-world-hunger-the-recovery-needs-to-start-soon-51629320042 ; Accessed on 1/01/23; © 2023 Dow Jones & Company, Inc.

Tucker, Jeffrey A; *Lockdown Suicide Data Reveal Predictable Tragedy*; May 22, 2020; https://www.aier.org/article/lockdown-suicide-data-reveal-predictable-tragedy/ ; Accessed on 1/01/23; © 2021 American Institute for Economic Research.

[20] Hennelly, Bob; *Many Deaths During the Pandemic Were Simply Due to Lack of Access to Health Care*; April 30, 2021; https://truthout.org/articles/many-deaths-during-the-pandemic-were-simply-due-to-lack-of-access-to-health-care/ ; Accessed on 1/01/23; © 2023 Truthout.

[21] *America's Frontline Doctors Are Being Censored*; July 28, 2020; https://freedomman.org/2020/americas-frontline-doctors-are-being-censored/ ; Accessed on 1/01/23; © 2016 - 2022 Freedom Man Press.

[22] Hegarty, Joe; *Democrats are the party of slavery, Jim Crow*; October 20, 2018; https://www.courierpostonline.com/story/opinion/readers/2018/10/20/democrats-party-slavery-jim-crow-joe-hegarty/1711669002/ ; Accessed on 1/01/23; © 2023 www.courierpostonline.com.

Bauer, Gary; *Has the Democratic Party become the party of abortion?*; May 7, 2015; https://www.foxnews.com/opinion/has-the-democratic-party-become-the-party-of-abortion ; Accessed on 1/01/23; ©2023 FOX News Network, LLC.

Manchester, Julia; *COVID-19 rules boomerang on Democrats*; 2/17/22; https://thehill.com/homenews/campaign/594603-democrats-face-blowback-over-covid-19-policies/ ; Accessed on 1/01/23; © 1998 - 2023 NEXSTAR MEDIA INC.

[23] Ohlers, R. Clinton; *Effectiveness of hydroxychloroquine was hiding in plain sight*; January 1, 2023; https://www.worldtribune.com/effectiveness-of-hydroxychloroquine-was-hiding-in-plain-sight/ © 2023, ↑ World Tribune: U.S. Politics and Culture, Geopolitics, Northeast Asia, China, Geostrategy-Direct, International Security, Corporate Watch, Media Watch.

[24] RT News; *Insider exposes Google's efforts to influence 2020 election against Trump*; June 24, 2019; https://www.rt.com/usa/462597-veritas-google-trump-fairness/ ; Accessed on 12/27/22; HomeUSA News.

[25] Ciaccia, Chris; *Former Facebook Exec Won't Let Own Kids Use Social Media, Says It's 'Destroying How Society Works'*; December 12, 2017; https://www.foxnews.com/tech/former-facebook-exec-wont-let-own-kids-use-social-media-says-its-destroying-how-society-works ; Accessed on 1/01/23; ©2023 FOX News Network, LLC.

Conard, Kristin; *The Real Reason Tech Moguls Don't Let Their Kids On Social Media*; December 6, 2021; https://www.thelist.com/677684/the-real-reason-tech-moguls-dont-let-their-kids-on-social-media/ ; Accessed on 1/01/23.

[26] Presented by AmericanFaith.com; Dr. Bryan Ardis Video (and written report): *Dr Bryan Ardis with the most stunning*

TRUTH about Covid, Fauci & Remdesivir you could never imagine: https://www.bitchute.com/video/IC2LQQpieYl6/ ; Accessed on 12/11/22; © 2022 Time to Free America.

[27] Ibid.

[28] Ibid.

[29] Becker's Hospital Review, *State-by-state breakdown of federal aid per COVID-19 case.* Kaiser Health News used a state breakdown provided to the House Ways and Means Committee by HHS along with COVID-19 cases tabulated by The New York Times for its analysis. https://www.beckershospitalreview.com/finance/state-by-state-breakdown-of-federal-aid-per-covid-19-case.html)* ; Accessed on 01/01/23; ©2023 Becker's Healthcare.

[30] H.R. 748 - CARES Act; https://www.congress.gov/bill/116th-congress/house-bill/748 ; Accessed on 12/27/22; Library of Congress.

[31] Lapin, Tamar; *Trump's Regeneron COVID-19 treatment tested using aborted fetal tissue cells*; October 8, 2020; https://nypost.com/2020/10/08/regeneron-covid-19-treatment-tested-using-aborted-fetal-tissue-cells/ ; Accessed on 12/27/22; © 2022 NYP Holdings, Inc.

[32] Presented by AmericanFaith.com; Dr. Bryan Ardis Video (and written report): *Dr Bryan Ardis with the most stunning TRUTH about Covid, Fauci & Remdesivir you could never imagine*: https://www.bitchute.com/video/IC2LQQpieYl6/ ; Accessed on 12/11/22; © 2022 Time to Free America.

CHAPTER 6 – FOX SNAKE FAUCI

[1] Stephen means garland or crown.
Wood, Henry; *50 Regal Baby Names That Mean "Crown"*; November 12, 2022; https://namesthatmean.com/baby-names-that-mean-crown/ ; Accessed on 1/01/23; © 2023 Names That Mean.

Anthony means priceless one or highly praiseworthy.
Garone, Sarah; *Anthony Name Meaning*; September 26, 2021; https://www.verywellfamily.com/anthony-name-meaning-origin-popularity-5119116 ; Accessed on 1/01/23; 2023; © Dotdash Media, Inc.

Fauci means sickle maker.
Fauci; https://babynames.com/name/fauci ; Accessed on 1/01/23; ©1996-2023 Moss Gathering LLC - Las Vegas, NV.

[2] Husebo, Wendell; *Fauci & NIH Take Heat over Funding of Gain-of-Function at Wuhan Lab: 'Will there be consequences?'*; October 21, 2021;

https://www.breibart.com/politics/2021/10/21/anthony-fauci-and-nih-take-heat-over-funding-of-gain-of-function-research-at-wuhan-lab-will-there-be-consequences/ ; Accessed on 1/01/23; ©BreibartNews.

[3] Definition of sickle: The word *sickle* is a noun and means: *An agricultural implement consisting of a curved metal blade with a short handle fitted on a tang*; https://www.merriam-webster.com/dictionary/sickle; Accessed on 1/01/23; © 2023 Merriam-Webster, Incorporated.

[4] Stephen means garland or crown.
Wood, Henry; *50 Regal Baby Names That Mean "Crown"*; November 12, 2022; https://namesthatmean.com/baby-names-that-mean-crown/ ; Accessed on 1/01/23; © 2023 Names That Mean.

Anthony means priceless one or highly praiseworthy.
Garone, Sarah; *Anthony Name Meaning*; September 26, 2021; https://www.verywellfamily.com/anthony-name-meaning-origin-popularity-5119116 ; Accessed on 1/01/23; 2023; © Dotdash Media, Inc.

Fauci means sickle maker.
Fauci; https://babynames.com/name/fauci ; Accessed on 1/01/23; ©1996-2023 Moss Gathering LLC - Las Vegas, NV.

[5] Post Editorial Board; *Fauci's agency admits it funded gain-of-function work in Wuhan: What else are they keeping from us?*; October 21, 2021; http://nypost.com/2021/10/21/faucis-agency-admits-it-funded-gain-of-function-work-in-wuhan-what-else-are-they-keeping-from-us/ ; Accessed on 1/01/23; © 2023 NYP Holdings, Inc.

[6] Dr. Joseph Mercola was quoted in Epoch Times, in an article on March 21, 2022: Hundreds of studies show lockdowns failed to meaningfully reduce Covid-19 deaths, while Covid-19 shot mandates are counterproductive and harmful… but eventually it will become widely known that, as Jeffrey Tucker, founder, and president of the Brownstone Institute, put it, 'these interventions turned a manageable pandemic into a catastrophe.' "
Analysis By Mercola, Dr. Joseph; *Did Lockdowns Cause Increased Mortality Rates?*; September 2, 2022; https://drjosephmercola.com/did-lockdowns-cause-increased-mortality-rates/ ; Accessed 1/01/23; © 2023 · Dr. Joseph Mercola.

[7] Van Elsland, Dr. Sabine L, O'Hare, Ryan; *COVID-19: Imperial researchers model likely impact of public health measures*; March 17. 2020; https://www.imperial.ac.uk/news/196234/covid-19-imperial-researchers-model-likely-impact/ ; Accessed on 1/01/23; © *Imperial College London.*

[8] Mayer, Rick; *A John Hopkins study says 'ill-founded' COVID lockdowns did more harm than good;* February 2, 2022; https://health.wusf.usf.edu/health-news-florida/2022-02-02/a-johns-hopkins-study-says-ill-founded-lockdowns-did-little-to-limit-covid-deaths ; Accessed 1/01/23; © 2022 Health News Florida.

[9] Maddow, Rachel; *Maddow: If You've Been Putting Off Vaccination, The Time To Do It Is Now;* December 21, 2021; https://youtu.be/tj6EkqfCRbA ; Accessed 1/01/23; MSNBC Online.

[10] Priority question for written answer P-003358/2022, to the Commission, Rule 138, Bernhard Zimniok (ID); *Implications of statement by Pfizer executive for COVID passport*; December 10, 2022; https://www.europarl.europa.eu/doceo/document/P-9-2022-003358_EN.html ; Accessed 1/01/23; European Parliament website.

[11] Samuels, Brett; Trump administration launches 'Operation Warp Speed' to accelerate vaccine development; 4/09/20; https://thehill.com/policy/healthcare/495315-trump-administration-pushing-for-accelerated-vaccine-development/ ; Accessed on 1/01/23; © 1998 - 2023 NEXSTAR MEDIA INC.

[12] Madej, Dr. Carrie, https://stopworldcontrol.com/madej/ ; Accessed on 1/11/23; © 2023 Stop World Control

CHAPTER 7 — DIAMONDBACK DEMOCRATS

[1] Swain, Carol; The Inconvenient Truth About the Democratic Party; May 21, 2017; https://www.prageru.com/video/the-inconvenient-truth-about-the-democratic-party ; Accessed on 12/27/22; © 2022 Prager University.

[2] On December 3, 1867, President Andrew Johnson said this in his annual message to Congress, "...Negroes have shown less capacity for government than any other race of people...barbarism." (This sentence can be found in context with the other quoted material in the 13th paragraph, in the 3rd sentence.); https://millercenter.org/the-presidency/presidential-speeches/december-3-1867-third-annual-message-congress ; Accessed on 12/27/22; © Copyright 2022. Rector and Visitors of the University of Virginia.

[3] Lambert, Laura; *Stockholm syndrome*; August 22, 2022; https://www.britannica.com/science/Stockholm-syndrome ; Accessed 1/01/23; ©Encyclopedia Britannica.

[4] Mueller, Marnie; *Wwii Reparations: Japanese American Internees*; February 18, 1999; https://www.democracynow.org/1999/2/18/wwii_reparations _japanese_american_internees ; Accessed on 12/27/22; ©democracynow.org.

[5] By the Investopedia Team; *Holocaust Restitution Payments*; September 27, 2021; https://www.investopedia.com/terms/h/holocaust-restitution-payments.asp ; Accessed on 1/01/23; Investopedia is part of the Dotdash Meredith publishing family.

[6] By the Post Editorial Board; Biden's lunatic bid to pay poor nations for climate reparations; November 21, 2022; https://nypost.com/2022/11/21/bidens-lunatic-bid-to-pay-poor-nations-for-climate-reparations/ ; Accessed on 1/01/23; © 2023 NYP Holdings, Inc.

[7] Myers, Barton; *Sherman's Field Order No. 15*; September 30, 2020; https://www.georgiaencyclopedia.org/articles/history-archaeology/shermans-field-order-no-15/ ; Accessed on 1/01/23; © 2004–2023 Georgia Humanities, University of Georgia Press.

[8] By Wallbuilders; *Abraham Lincoln Portrait and Emancipation Proclamation*; December 31, 2022; https://wallbuiders.com/abraham-lincoln-portrait-emancipation-proclamation/ ; Accessed on 1/01/23; Copyright 2021 WallBuilders.

[9] Gates Jr., Henry Louis; *The Truth Behind '40 Acres and a Mule'*; https://www.pbs.org/wnet/african-americans-many-rivers-to-cross/history/the-truth-behind-40-acres-and-a-mule/ ; Accessed on 1/01/23; © 2013 WNET.

[10] Author Unknown; *Plato's Cave: Bonhoeffer on Stupidity (entire quote)*; Date Unknown; https://www.platoscave.org/2021/10/bonhoeffer-on-stupidity-entire-quote.html ; Accessed on 1/01/23; Back on Twitter at @platoscavenews.

[11] Ballotpedia features 392,372 encyclopedic articles written and curated by our professional staff of editors, writers, and researchers; *Ballot harvesting (ballot collection) laws by state*; May 2022; https://ballotpedia.org/ballot_harvesting_(ballot_collection)_laws_by_state ; Accessed on 1/01/23; ©Ballotpedia.

[12] Kengor, Paul; *How Barack Obama Fundamentally Transformed the United States*; January 12, 2017; https://www.ncregister.com/news/how-barack-obama-fundamentally-transformed-the-united-states ; Accessed on 1/01/23.

[13] Steff S.; *Transgender broke weightlifting records by winning 2 medals in IWF*; December 7, 2017; https://nordiclifting.com/blogs/fitness/transgender-broke-weightlifting-records-by-winning-2-medals-in-iwf ; Accessed on 1/01/23; © Nordic Lifting 2013 – 2023.

[14] Starr, Penny; *Transgender MMA Fighter Who Fractured a Woman's Skull, Named 'Bravest Athlete in History'*; January 22,

2020; https://www.breitbart.com/sports/2020/01/22/transgender-mma-fighter-who-fractured-womans-skull-named-bravest-athlete-history/ ; Accessed on 1/01/23; © Breitbart News.

[15] Clement, Samuel; Transgender Prisoner Demitrius Minor Admits to Impregnating Two Inmates at All-Women's Jail; April 15, 2022; https://blacksportsonline.com/2022/04/transgender-prisoner-demitrius-minor-admits-to-impregnating-two-inmates-at-all-womens-jail/ ; Accessed on 1/01/23; Copyright © 2022 BSO Entertainment LLC.

[16] Colton, Emma; *Retired Navy SEAL made famous after coming out as a trans announces detransition: 'Destroyed my life';* December 11, 2022; https://www.foxnews.com/us/retired-navy-seal-made-famous-coming-out-trans-announces-detransition-destroyed-my-life ; Accessed on 1/01/23; ©2023 FOX News Network, LLC.

CHAPTER 8 – FIERY SERPENTS

[1] *Fiery* is the Hebrew word *saraph* H8314 from H8313; and it means *burning,* for example (figuratively) *poisonous (serpent);* specifically, *a saraph or symbolical creature (from their copper color):—fiery (serpent),* and *seraph;* Blue Letter Bible online: https://www.blueletterbible.org/lexicon/h8314/kjv/wlc/0-1/ ; Accessed on 1/01/23; ©2023 Blue Letter Bible.

[2] *Serpent* is the Hebrew word *nakas* H5175 (naw-khawsh'); from H5172 and it means a snake (from its hiss):—serpent. Blue Letter Bible online: https://www.blueletterbible.org/lexicon/h5175/kjv/wlc/0-1/ ; Accessed on 7/29/22; ©2022 Blue Letter Bible.

[3] *Swallow* is the Hebrew word *bala (baw-lah)* H1104 and it is a primitive root that means *to make away with (specifically by swallowing); generally, to destroy:*—*cover, destroy, devour, eat up, be at end, spend up,* and *swallow down (up);* Blue Letter Bible online: https://www.blueletterbible.org/lexicon/h1104/kjv/wlc/0-1/ ; Accessed on 1/01/23; ©2023 Blue Letter Bible.

CHAPTER 9 – SNAKE VENOM

[2] Brandt, Rosemary; Like Venom Coursing Through the Body: Researchers Identify Mechanism Driving COVID-19 Mortality; August 24, 2021; https://news.arizona.edu/story/venom-coursing-through-body-researchers-identify-mechanism-driving-covid-19-mortality ; Accessed on 1/01/23; © 2023 The Arizona Board of Regents on behalf of The University of Arizona.

[3] Michael Petro interviews Dr. Bryan Ardis; Dr. Bryan Ardis – Four Key Supplements Discovered to Neutralize COVID-19 Venom Protein; September 1, 2022; (Audio at about 7 minutes) https://omny.fm/shows/the-voice-of-healing-radio-apostle-michael-petro/dr-bryan-ardis-four-key-supplements-discovered-to ; Accessed on 1/01/23; © 2023 121cast Pty Ltd.

www.romelduanemooresr.com

808-371-0597